بسم الله الرحمن الرحيم

ADVICE ON ESTABLISHING AN ISLĀMIC HOME

"The likeness of a house in which Allāh is remembered and the house in which Allāh is not remembered is that of the living and the dead, respectively."

ADVICE ON ESTABLISHING AN ISLĀMIC HOME

by

Muḥammad Ṣāliḥ al-Munajjid

Dār as-Sunnah Publishers

B I R M I N G H A M

Second Edition Published in Great Britain, December 2013 / Muharram1435H
by Dār as-Sunnah Publishers

دار السنة
DĀR AS-SUNNAH PUBLISHERS
P.O. Box 9818, Birmingham, B11 4WA, United Kingdom

W: www.darassunnah.com
E: info@darassunnah.com
E: daar-us-sunnah@mail.com

British Library Cataloguing in publication Data.
A catalogue record for this book is available from the British Library.

Title: Advice on establishing an Islāmic Home
by: Muḥammad Ṣāliḥ al-Munajjid

ISBN 1-904336-07-8
Paper-back

First Edition 1423 AH/2003 CE
Second Edition 1435 AH / 2013 CE
Typeset by: Dār as-Sunnah Publishers

CONTENT

Introduction

All praise be to Allāh, we praise Him and seek His help and forgiveness. We seek refuge with Allāh from the evil of our own selves and from our evil deeds. Whomsoever Allāh guides, no one can lead astray, and whomsoever Allāh leaves astray, no one can guide. I bear witness that there is no god but Allāh Alone, with no partner or associate, and I bear witness that Muḥammad is His slave and Messenger.

The home is a blessing

Allāh says:

وَٱللَّهُ جَعَلَ لَكُم مِّنۢ بُيُوتِكُمْ سَكَنًا

And Allāh has made for you in your homes an abode...

[*al-Naḥl* (16) : 80]

Ibn Kathir said: 'Here Allāh, may He be blessed and exalted, is mentioning His complete blessing to His slaves: He has given them homes which are a peaceful abode for them, to which they retreat as a haven which covers them and gives them all kinds of benefits.'

What does the home represent to each one of us? Is it not the place where he eats, enjoys intimacy with his wife, sleeps and rests? Is it not the place where he can be alone and can meet with his wife and children?

Is the home not the place that offers cover and protection to women? Allāh tells us:

وَقَرْنَ فِي بُيُوتِكُنَّ وَلَا تَبَرَّجْنَ تَبَرُّجَ ٱلْجَٰهِلِيَّةِ ٱلْأُولَىٰ

And stay in your houses, and do not display yourselves like that of the times of ignorance...

[*al-Aḥzāb* (33) : 33]

If you think about those who are homeless, who live in shelters, or on the streets, or as refugees scattered in temporary camps, then you will realize the blessing of having a home. If you listen to a distressed homeless person saying, 'I have nowhere to settle, no fixed place to stay. Sometimes I sleep in so and so's house, sometimes in a cafe or park or on the sea-front, and I keep my clothes in my car', then you will realize the disruption that results from not having the blessing of a home.

When Allāh punished the Jews of *Banu Nadir*, He took away this blessing and expelled them from their homes, as He said:

هُوَ ٱلَّذِىٓ أَخْرَجَ ٱلَّذِينَ كَفَرُوا۟ مِنْ أَهْلِ ٱلْكِتَٰبِ مِن دِيَٰرِهِمْ لِأَوَّلِ ٱلْحَشْرِ

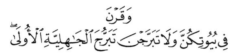

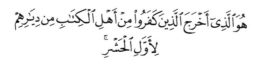

He it is Who drove out the disbelievers among the people of the Scripture (i.e. the Jews of the tribe of *Banu al-Nadir*) from their homes at the first gathering.

Then He said:

يُخْرِبُونَ بُيُوتَهُم بِأَيْدِيهِمْ وَأَيْدِي الْمُؤْمِنِينَ
فَاعْتَبِرُوا يَا أُولِي الْأَبْصَارِ ﴿٢﴾

...they destroyed their own dwellings with their own hands and the hands of the believers. Then take admonition, O you with eyes (to see).

[*al-Ḥashr* (59) : 2]

There are many motives for the believer to pay attention to putting his house in order.

[i]. Protecting himself and his family from the Fire of Hell, and keeping them safe from the burning punishment:

يَا أَيُّهَا الَّذِينَ آمَنُوا قُوا أَنفُسَكُمْ وَأَهْلِيكُمْ
نَارًا وَقُودُهَا النَّاسُ وَالْحِجَارَةُ عَلَيْهَا مَلَائِكَةٌ غِلَاظٌ شِدَادٌ
لَّا يَعْصُونَ اللَّهَ مَا أَمَرَهُمْ وَيَفْعَلُونَ مَا يُؤْمَرُونَ ﴿٦﴾

O you who believe! Ward off from yourselves and your families a Fire (Hell) whose fuel is men and stones, over which are (appointed) angels stern (and) severe, who disobey not, (from executing) the Commands they receive from Allāh, but do that which they are commanded.

[*al-Taḥrīm* (66) : 6]

[ii]. The great responsibility borne by the head of the household on the Day of Reckoning.

The Prophet (ﷺ) said:

> "Allāh will ask every shepherd (or responsible person) about his flock (those for whom he was responsible), whether he took care of it or neglected it, until He asks a man about his household."

[iii]. The home is a place to protect oneself, to keep away from evil and to keep ones own evil away from people. It is the refuge prescribed by Islām at times of *fitnah* (strife, tribulation).

The Prophet (ﷺ) said:

> "Blessed is the one who controls his tongue, whose house is sufficient for him, and who weeps over his mistakes."

The Prophet (ﷺ) said:

> "There are five things, whoever does one of them, Allāh will be with him: visiting the sick, going out for *jihād*, entering upon his leader with the intention of rebuking and respecting him, or sitting in his home so that the people are safe from him and he is safe from the people."

The Prophet (ﷺ) said:

> "The safety of a man at times of *fitnah* is in his staying home."

The Muslim can see the benefit of this advice when he is residing in a foreign land where he is unable to change much of the evil around him. Then he will have a refuge which, when he enters it, will protect him from doing *harām* things or looking at *harām* things, and will protect his wife from wanton display and unveiling, and will protect his children from bad company.

[iv]. People usually spend most of their time at home, especially when it is very hot or very cold, when it is raining, early or late in the day, and after finishing work or school, so this time should be spent in worship and *halāl* pursuits, otherwise it will be spent in wrongdoing.

[v]. And most importantly, paying attention to the home is the most important means of building a Muslim society, because the society is formed of the households and families that form its building blocks. Households form neighbourhoods, and neighbourhoods form societies. If the building blocks are sound, the society will be based on the laws of Allāh, standing firm in the face of enemies and filled with goodness that evil cannot penetrate. Then Muslim homes will produce pillars of society who will reform and guide it aright, such as exemplary callers, seekers of knowledge, sincere *mujāhidīn*, righteous wives, caring mothers and all other types of reformers.

Because this subject is so important, and our homes are full of so many shortcomings and evils and examples of negligence, this begs the very important question:

What are the means of reforming our homes?

The following contains advice on this topic. May Allāh benefit us from it, and cause the Muslims to focus their efforts on reviving the Muslim home.

All the following advice revolves around two things: achieving our interests, which is by establishing that which is right and good, and warding off evil, by removing that which can cause it or bring it into our homes.

[10] *Āli 'Imrān* (3): 195

FORMING THE HOUSEHOLD

Making a good choice when choosing a wife

وَأَنكِحُوا۟ ٱلْأَيَـٰمَىٰ مِنكُمْ وَٱلصَّـٰلِحِينَ مِنْ عِبَادِكُمْ وَإِمَآئِكُمْ ۚ إِن
يَكُونُوا۟ فُقَرَآءَ يُغْنِهِمُ ٱللَّهُ مِن فَضْلِهِۦ ۗ وَٱللَّهُ وَٰسِعٌ عَلِيمٌ ﴿٣٢﴾

And marry those among you who are single and (also marry) the *ṯālihṯn* (pious) of your (male) slaves and maid-servants (female slaves). If they be poor, Allāh will enrich them out of His Bounty. And Allāh is All-Sufficient for His creatures needs, All-Knowing.

[*al-Nūr* (24) : 32]

The head of the household must select a righteous and suitable wife based on the following conditions described in various *aḥādīth*:

> "A woman may be married for four things: her wealth, her lineage, her beauty or her religion. Choose the one who is religious, may your hands be rubbed with dust [i.e., may you prosper]!" [1]

---

[1] Reported by Bukhārī and Muslim

> "This world is all temporary conveniences, and the greatest joy in this life is a righteous wife." [2]

> "Let every one of you have a thankful heart, a remembering tongue [remembering Allāh] and a believing wife who will help him with regard to the Hereafter." [3]

According to another report:

> "A righteous wife to help you with your worldly and religious affairs is the best treasure anyone could have." [4]

> "Marry one who is loving and fertile, for I will be proud before the other Prophets of your great numbers on the Day of Resurrection." [5]

> "I advise you to marry virgins, for their wombs are more fresh, their mouths are more sweet and they are more content with little."

According to another report:

> "...and they are less likely to deceive." [6]

---

[2] Reported by Muslim, [1468].

[3] Reported by Aḥmad, [5/282], and al-Tirmidhī and ibn Mājah from Thawbān. *Ṣaḥīḥ al-Jāmi'*, [5231].

[4] Reported by al-Bayhaqī, *Ṣaḥīḥ al-Jāmi'*, [4285].

[5] Reported by Aḥmad, *Ṣaḥīḥ al-Irwā'*, [6/195].

[6] Reported by ibn Mājah, *al-Silsilah al-Ṣaḥīḥah*, [623].

Just as a righteous wife is one of the four elements of happiness, so a bad wife is one of the four elements of misery, as it says in the ṣaḥīḥ ḥadīth:

> "One of (the elements of) happiness is a righteous wife, who when you see her you feel pleased, and when you are away, you feel that you can trust her with regard to herself and your property. And one of (the elements of) misery is a bad wife who when you see her, you feel upset, she keeps attacking you verbally, and when you are away, you do not feel that you can trust her with regard to herself and your property."

On the other hand, it is also essential to look at the situation of the prospective husband who is proposing marriage to the Muslim woman, and to agree to his proposal in accordance with the following conditions:

The Prophet (ﷺ) said:

> "If there comes to you one with whose religion and character you are pleased, then marry your daughter [or sister, etc.] to him, otherwise there will be fitnah and great corruption in the land."

All of the above must be achieved through asking the right questions, verifying facts, gathering information and checking sources, so that the home will not be corrupted or destroyed.

The righteous man and righteous woman together will build a righteous home, because

وَٱلْبَلَدُ ٱلطَّيِّبُ يَخْرُجُ نَبَاتُهُۥ بِإِذْنِ رَبِّهِۦ ۖ وَٱلَّذِى خَبُثَ لَا يَخْرُجُ
إِلَّا نَكِدًا ۚ كَذَٰلِكَ نُصَرِّفُ ٱلْءَايَٰتِ لِقَوْمٍ يَشْكُرُونَ ﴿٥٨﴾

The vegetation of a good land comes forth (easily) by the Permission of its Lord, and that which is bad, brings forth nothing but a little with difficulty...

[*al-A'rāf* (7) : 58]

Striving to guide one's wife

If one's wife is righteous, this is a blessing indeed, and this is from the Bounty of Allāh. If she is not that righteous, then it is the duty of the head of the household to strive to guide her. Any of the following scenarios may apply:

A man may marry a woman who is not religious in the first place, because he himself is not religious at first, or he may have married her in the hope of guiding her, or under pressure from his relatives, for example. In these cases he must strive hard to guide her.

A man must also realize from the outset that guidance comes from Allāh, and that Allāh is the One Who reforms people. One of His blessings to his slave Zakariyah was, as He said:

وَأَصْلَحْنَا لَهُۥ زَوْجَهُۥٓ ۚ إِنَّهُمْ

...**and [We] cured his wife for him...**

[*al-Anbiya'* (21) : 90]

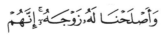

This curing or reforming may have been physical or religious.

Ibn 'Abbās said:

> "She was barren and could not have children, then she had a child."

'Atā' said:

> "She was harsh of tongue, and Allāh reformed her."

There are various means of guiding or reforming one's wife, such as:

- Paying attention to correcting her worship of Allāh in all its aspects, as will be discussed in detail below.
- Striving to strengthen her eemaan, such as:
- encouraging her to pray at night (*qiyām al-layl*)
- encouraging her to read Qur'ān
- encouraging her to memorize adhkār and remember the appropriate times and occasions for saying them
- encouraging her to give charity
- encouraging her to read useful Islāmic books
- encouraging her to listen to useful Islāmic cassettes that can increase knowledge and strengthen *īmān* - and continuing to supply her with them.

- choosing good, religious friends for her, with whom she can form ties of sisterhood and have good conversations and purposeful visits.

- protecting her from evil and blocking off all avenues for it to reach her, by keeping her away from bad companions and bad places.

CREATING AN ATMOSPHERE OF FAITH IN THE HOME

Making the home a place for the remembrance of Allāh

The Prophet (ﷺ) said:

> "The likeness of a house in which Allāh is remembered and the house in which Allāh is not remembered is that of the living and the dead, respectively."

We must make our homes places where Allāh is remembered in all kinds of ways, whether in our hearts, verbally, during prayer, by reading Qur'ān, by discussing Islāmic issues, or by reading different kinds of Islāmic books.

How many Muslim homes nowadays are dead because there is no remembrance of Allāh, as mentioned in the *ḥadīth*. What must they be like when all that is heard therein is the music of *Shayṭān* with instruments and singing, and backbiting, slander and gossip?

What must they be like when they are filled with evil and sin, such as the *harām* mixing of the sexes and wanton display between relatives who are not *mahram* or with neighbours who enter the home?

How can the angels enter a home like this? Revive your homes with all kinds of *dhikr*, may Allāh have mercy on you!

Make your homes as a place of worship

What is meant is taking the home as a place of worship? Allāh says:

وَأَوْحَيْنَآ إِلَىٰ مُوسَىٰ وَأَخِيهِ
أَن تَبَوَّءَا لِقَوْمِكُمَا بِمِصْرَ بُيُوتًا وَٱجْعَلُوا۟ بُيُوتَكُمْ قِبْلَةً
وَأَقِيمُوا۟ ٱلصَّلَوٰةَ ۗ وَبَشِّرِ ٱلْمُؤْمِنِينَ ﴿٨٧﴾

And We inspired Mūsā and his brother (saying): 'Take dwellings for your people in Egypt, and make your dwellings as places for your worship, and perform *al-ṭalāh*, and give glad tidings to the believers.'

[*Yūnus* (10) : 87]

Ibn 'Abbās said:

> 'They were commanded to take their dwellings as places of prayer [lit. *masjid*].'

Ibn Kathīr said:

'This - and Allāh knows best - was because of the intensity of the tribulation that they were facing from Pharaoh and his people. They were commanded to pray much, as Allāh says:

يَٰٓأَيُّهَا ٱلَّذِينَ
ءَامَنُوا۟ ٱسْتَعِينُوا۟ بِٱلصَّبْرِ وَٱلصَّلَوٰةِ ۚ إِنَّ ٱللَّهَ مَعَ ٱلصَّٰبِرِينَ ﴿١٥٣﴾

O you who believe! Seek help with patience and prayer...

[*al-Baqarah* 2:153],

And as it was reported in the *ḥadīth* that the Messenger of Allāh (ﷺ), when he was distressed by something, would pray."

This explains the importance of worshipping at home, especially at times when the Muslims are in a position of weakness, as happens in some places where the Muslims cannot pray openly in front of the *kuffār*. In this context we may think of the *miḥrāb* of Maryam, which was her place of worship, as Allāh says:

كُلَّمَا دَخَلَ عَلَيْهَا زَكَرِيَّا ٱلْمِحْرَابَ وَجَدَ عِندَهَا رِزْقًا ۖ

...Every time Zakariyah entered the *miḥrāb* to visit her, he found her supplied with sustenance...

[*Āli 'Imrān* (3) : 37]

The Companions (may Allāh be pleased with them) used to be keen to pray at home - apart from the fard or obligatory prayers (which they prayed in congregation in the *masjid*) - and there is a moving story concerning this.

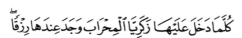

Maḥmūd ibn al-Rabi' al-Anṣārī reported that 'Utban ibn Mālik - who was one of the Companions of the Messenger (ﷺ) and was one of the Anṣār who had been present at *Badr* - came to the Messenger of Allāh (ﷺ) and said:

> "I am losing my sight, and I lead my people in prayer. When it rains, the valley between me and them gets flooded and I cannot get to their *masjid* to lead them in prayer. O Messenger of Allāh, I would like you to come and pray in my house so that I can take it as a place for prayer."

The Messenger of Allāh (ﷺ) said:

> "I will do that, *inshā'Allāh*. 'Utbān said: 'The next day the Messenger of Allāh (ﷺ) and Abū Bakr came in the morning. The Messenger of Allāh (ﷺ) asked for permission to enter, and I gave him permission. He did not sit down until he entered the house, then he said, 'Where would you like me to pray in your house?' I showed him a corner of the house, then the Messenger of Allāh (ﷺ) stood up, said *takbīr*, and we stood in a row behind him, and he prayed two rak'āhs and gave the *salām* at the end of the prayer." [1]

---

[1] Reported by al-Bukhārī, *al-Fatḥ*, [1/519].

Spiritual training for the members of the household

'Ā'ishah (may Allāh be pleased with her) said:

> "The Messenger of Allāh (ﷺ) used to pray *qiyām* at night, and when he prayed *witr* he would say, 'Get up and pray witr, O 'Ā'ishah'" [2]

The Prophet (ﷺ) said:

> "May Allāh have mercy on a man who gets up at night and prays, then he wakes up his wife to pray, and if she refuses he throws water in her face." [3]

Encouraging the women of one's household to give charity is another means of increasing faith. This is something very important which the Prophet (ﷺ) encouraged, when he said,

> "O women! Give in charity, for I have seen that you form the majority of the inhabitants of Hell." [4]

One of the new ideas is to have a box at home for donations to the poor and needy: whatever is put in the box belongs to them, because it is their vessel in the Muslim home.

If the family members see an example among them fasting on

---

2 Reported by Muslim, *Muslim bi Sharḥ al-Nawāwī*, [6/23].

3 Reported by Aḥmad and Abū Dāwūd. *Ṣaḥīḥ al-Jāmi'*, [3488].

4 Reported by al-Bukhārī, *al-Fatḥ*, [1/405].

al-Ayyām al-Bīd (the 13th, 14th and 15th of each *Hijrī* month), Mondays and Thursdays, *Tāsū'ā'* and *'Ashūra'* (the 9th and 10th of *Muḥarram*), *'Arafah*, and frequently in *Muḥarram* and *Sha'bān*, this will be a motive for them to do likewise.

Paying attention to *adhkār* and Sunnah *du'ā's* that have to do with the home

Adkhār for entering the home

Muslim reported in his *Ṣaḥīḥ* that the Messenger of Allāh (ﷺ) said:

> "When any one of you enters his home and mentions the Name of Allāh when he enters and when he eats, the *Shayṭān* says: 'You have no place to stay and nothing to eat here.' If he enters and does not mention the name of Allāh when he enters, [the *Shayṭān*] says, 'You have a place to stay.' If he does not mention the name of Allāh when he eats, [the *Shayṭān* says], 'You have a place to stay and something to eat.'" [5]

Abū Dāwūd reported in his *Sunan* that the Messenger of Allāh (ﷺ) said:

> "If a man goes out of his house and says,
>
> «بِسْمِ اللهِ، تَوَكَّلْتُ عَلَى اللهِ، وَلَا حَوْلَ وَلَا قُوَّةَ إِلَّا بِاللهِ»

[5] Reported by Imām Aḥmad , *al-Musnad*, [3/346]; Muslim, [3/1599].

"Bismillāh, tawakkaltu 'alā Allāh, lā ḥawla wa lāquwwata illā billāh."

"In the name of Allāh, I put my trust in Allāh, there is no help and no strength except in Allāh,"

it will be said to him, 'This will take care of you, you are guided, you have what you need and you are protected.' The *Shayṭān* will stay away from him, and another *Shayṭān* will say to him, 'What can you do with a man who is guided, provided for and protected?'" [6]

Siwāk

Imām Muslim reported in his *Ṣaḥīḥ* that 'Ā'ishah *'Umm al-Mu'minīn* (may Allāh be pleased with her) said:

"When the Messenger of Allāh (ﷺ) entered his house, the first thing he would do was use *siwāk*." [7]

[6] Reported by Abū Dāwūd and al-Tirmidhī. *Ṣaḥīḥ al-Jāmi'*, [no. 499].

[7] Reported by Muslim, [no. 44].

Continuously reciting *Sūrah al-Baqarah* in the house to ward off the *Shayṭān*

There are a number of *aḥādīth* concerning this, such as:

The Messenger of Allāh (ﷺ) said:

> "Do not make your houses into graves. The *Shayṭān* flees from a house in which *Sūrah al-Baqarah* is recited." [8]

The Messenger of Allāh (ﷺ) said:

> "Recite *Sūrah al-Baqarah* in your houses, for the *Shayṭān* does not enter a house in which *Sūrah al-Baqarah* is recited." [9]

Concerning the virtues of the last two *āyāt* of this *Sūrah*, and the effect of reciting them in ones house, he (ﷺ) said:

> "Allāh wrote a document two thousand years before He created the heavens and the earth, which is kept near the Throne, and He revealed two *āyāt* of it with which He concluded *Sūrah al-Baqarah*. If they are recited in a house for three consecutive nights, the *Shayṭān* will not approach it." [10]

---

[8] Reported by Muslim, [1/539]

[9] Reported by al-Ḥākim in *al-Mustadrak*. [1/561]; *Ṣaḥīḥ al-Jāmi'*, [1170].

[10] Reported by Imām Aḥmad in *al-Musnad*, [4/274], and others. *Ṣaḥīḥ al-Jāmi'*, [1799].

ISLĀMIC KNOWLEDGE IN THE HOME

Teaching the family

This is an obligation which the head of the household must undertake, in obedience to the command of Allāh:

يَٰٓأَيُّهَا ٱلَّذِينَ ءَامَنُواْ قُوٓاْ أَنفُسَكُمۡ وَأَهۡلِيكُمۡ
نَارٗا وَقُودُهَا ٱلنَّاسُ وَٱلۡحِجَارَةُ عَلَيۡهَا مَلَٰٓئِكَةٌ غِلَاظٞ شِدَادٞ

O you who believe! Ward off from yourselves and your families a Fire (Hell) whose fuel is men and stones...

[*al-Taḥrīm* 66:6]

This *āyāh* is the basic principle regarding the teaching and upbringing of ones family, and enjoining them to do what is good and forbidding them to do what is evil. There follow some of the comments of the *mufassirīn* on this *āyāh*, in so far as it pertains to the duties of the head of the household.

Qatādah said:

> 'He should command them to obey Allāh, and forbid them to disobey Him, and direct them in accordance with the commands of Allāh, and help them to do that.'

Daḥḥak and Muqatil said:

> 'It is the Muslim's duty to teach his family, including relatives and female slaves, what Allāh has enjoined upon them and what He has forbidden.'

'Alī (may Allāh be pleased with him) said:

> 'Teach them and discipline them.'

al-Ṭabarī said:

> 'We must teach our children and wives the religion and goodness, and whatever they need of good manners. If the Messenger of Allāh (ﷺ) used to urge the teaching of female servants, who were slaves, what do you think about your children and wives, who are free?'

al-Bukhārī said in his *Ṣaḥīḥ*: 'Chapter: a man's teaching his female slaves and wife.' Then he quoted the *ḥadīth* of the Prophet (ﷺ):

> 'There are three who will have two rewards: ...a man who has a female slave whom he teaches good manners and teaches her well, and teaches her knowledge, and teaches her well, then he frees her and marries her: he will have two rewards.'

Ibn Hajr said, commenting on this *hadith*:

> 'The chapter heading refers specifically to female slaves, and to wives by analogy, i.e., teaching one's free wife about her duties towards Allāh and the Sunnah of His Messenger is more clearly essential than teaching one's female slaves.'

In the midst of all a man's activities, work and other commitments, he may forget to allow himself time for teaching his wife. One solution to this is to allocate some time for the family, and even for others such as relatives, to hold a study-circle at home. He can let everyone know the time and encourage them to come regularly, so that it will be an ongoing commitment for him and for them. Something similar happened at the time of the Prophet (ﷺ).

al-Bukhārī said:

> 'Chapter: can the women be given a day exclusively for them to seek knowledge?, and quoted the *ḥadīth* of Abū Sa'īd al-Khudrī (may Allāh be pleased with him): 'The women said to the Prophet (ﷺ): 'The men always crowd us out and we cannot reach you, so set aside a day for us when we can come to you.' So he set aside a day when he would meet them and teach them.'

Ibn Hajr said:

> 'A similar report was narrated by Ṣaḥl ibn Abī Sāliḥ from Abū Hurayrah, according to which [the Prophet

(ﷺ)] said: 'Your appointment is in the house of so and so,' and he came to them and spoke to them.'

What we learn from this is that women should be taught in their houses, and we see how keen the women of the Companion were to learn. Directing teaching efforts to men alone, and not to women, is a serious shortcoming on the part of daiṝyahs and heads of households.

Some readers may ask, suppose we set aside a day, and tell our families about it - what should we study in these gatherings? Where do we begin? I suggest that you begin with a simple program to teach your family in general, and the women in particular, using the following books:

The *tafsīr* of *al-'Allāmah* Ibn Sa'di, entitled *Taysīr al-Karīm al-Raḥmān fi Tafsīr Kalām al-Mannān*, which is published in seven volumes and is written in an easy style; you can read it or teach somes surahs and passages from it.

Riyaḍ al-Ṣālihīn - you could discuss the *aḥādīth* quoted, along with the footnotes and the lessons learned from them.

You could also refer to the book *Nuẓhāt al-Muṭṭāqīn.*

Ḥasan al-Uswah bima thubita 'an Allāhi wa Rasūlihi fi'l-Nuswah, by *al-'Allāmah* Ṣiddiq Ḥasan Khan.

It is also important to teach women some of the *aḥkām* of fiqh, such as the rulings on *tahārah* (purity) and menstrual and post-partum bleeding, *ṣalāh*, *ẓakāh*, *siyām* (fasting) and *ḥajj*, if she is able to go; some of the rulings on food and drink, clothing and adornment, the *sunan al-fitrah*, rulings on *maḥarim* (who is a *mahram* relative and who is not), rulings on singing and photography, and so on. Among the important sources of such information are the *fatwas* (rulings or vedicts) of the scholars, such as the collections of *fatwas* by Shaykh 'Abd al-'Azīz ibn Baz and Shaykh Muḥammad ibn Ṣāliḥ al-'Uthaymīn, and other scholars, whether they are written *fatwas* or *fatwas* recorded on tapes.

Another matter that may be included in a syllabus for teaching women and family members is reminding them of lessons or public lectures given by trustworthy scholars and seekers of knowledge which they can attend, so they can have a variety of excellent sources for learning. We should not forget either the radio programs of *Idha'āt al-Qur'ān al-Karīm*; another means of teaching is reminding family members of the particular days when women can attend Islāmic bookstores, and taking them there, within the guidelines of *sharī'ah* [i.e., proper *hijab*, etc.]

Start building an Islāmic 'library' in your home

Another thing that will help in teaching your family and letting them develop a understanding of their religion and help them adhere to its rules, is having ones own Islāmic library at home. It does not have to be extensive; what matters is choosing good books, putting them in a place where they are readily accessible, and encouraging family members to read them.

You could put books in a clean and tidy corner of the living room, and in a suitable place in a bedroom or guest room; this will make it easy for any member of the family to read constantly.

In order to build a library properly - and Allāh loves things to be done properly - you should include references so that family members can research various matters and children can use them for their studies. You should also include books of varying levels, so that old and young, men and women can all use them. You should also have books for giving to guests, childrens friends and family visitors, but try to get books that are attractively presented, edited properly and with the sources and classification of the *aḥādīth* properly given. You can make the most of Islamic bookstores and exhibitions to build a home library, after consulting and seeking advice from those who have experience in the field of books. One way in which you can help family members to find a book when they want it is to organize the books according to subject, with books of *Tafsīr* on one shelf, books of *ḥadīth* on another, *fiqh* on a third, and so on. One of the family members could also compile alphabetical or subject indexes of the library, to make it easier to look for books.

Many of those who want to start a home library may ask for titles of Islāmic books. Here are a few suggestions:

Tafsīr:

Tafsīr Ibn Kathīr
Tafsīr Ibn Sa'di
Zubdāt al-Tafsīr by al-Ashkar
Bada'i' al-Tafsīr by Ibn al-Qayyim
Usūl al-Tafsīr by Ibn 'Uthaymin
Lamahāt fi 'Ulūm al-Qur'ān by Muḥammad al-Sabbagh

Ḥadīth:

Ṣaḥīḥ al-Kalim al-Tayyib
'Aml al-Muslim fi'l-Yawm wa'l-Laylah (or: *Al-Ṣaḥīḥ al-Musnad min Adhkār al-Yawm wa'l-Laylah*)
Riyaḍ al-Ṣālihīn and its commentary *Nuzhāt al-Muṭṭāqīn*
Mukhtasar Ṣaḥīḥ al-Bukharī by al-Zubaydī
Mukhtasar Ṣaḥīḥ Muslim by al-Mundhirī and al-Albānī
Ṣaḥīḥ al-Jami' al-Saghīr
Da'īf al-Jami' al-Saghīr
Ṣaḥīḥ al-Targhīb wa'l-Tarhīb
Al-Sunnah wa Makanatuha fi'l-Tashri'
Qawa'id wa fawa'id min al-Arba'īn al-Nawawiyyah by Nazim Sultan

'Aqīdah:

Fatḥ al-Majīd Sharḥ Kitāb al-Tawḥīd (edited by al-Arna'ūt)
A'lām al-Sunnah al-Manshūrah by al-Hakamī (ed.)
Sharḥ al-'Aqīdah al-Tahhawīyyah, edited by al-Albānī
The series on 'Aqīdah by 'Umar Sulaymān al-Ashqar in 8 parts [also available in English translation]
Ashrāt al-Sa'ah by Dr. Yūsuf al-Wābil

Fiqh:

Manār al-Sabīl by Ibn Duwiyyān
Irwā' al-Ghalīl by al-Albānī
Zād al-Ma'ad
al-Mughnī by Ibn Qudamah

Fiqh al-Sunnah [also available in English translation]
Al-Mulakhkhas al-Fiqhī by Sālih al-Fawzān
Collections of fatwas by different scholars ('Abd al-'Azīz ibn Baz, Muḥammad Sāliḥ al-'Uthaymin, 'Abd-Allāh ibn Jibrīn)
Sifāt Salāh al-Nabi (peace and blessings of Allāh be upon him) by Shaykh al-Albānī and Shaykh 'Abd al-'Azīz ibn Baz [available in English under the title *The Prophet's Prayer Described*]
Mukhtasar Aḥkām al-Janā'iz by al-Albānī.

Good manners and purification of the soul:

Taḥdhib Madārij al-Sālikīn
Al-Fawā'id
Al-Jawab al-Kāfi
Tariq al-Hijratayn wa Bāb al-Sa'adatayn
Al-Wābil al-Sayib
Rafiṛ al-Kalim al-Tayyib by Ibn al-Qayyim
Lata'if al-Ma'arif by Ibn Rajab
Taḥdhib Maw'iẓāt al-Mu'minīn
Ghadha' al-Albab

Sīrah and biographies:

Al-Bidayah wa'l-Niḥayah by Ibn Kathīr
Mukhtasar al-Shama'il al-Muḥammadiyyah by al-Tirmidhī, abridged by al-Albānī
Al-Raḥiq al-Makḥtūm by al-Mubarakpoori [available in English translation]
Al-'Awasim min al-Qawasim by Ibn al-'Arabi, ed. by al-

Khatib and al-Istanbūli
Al-Mujtamā' al-Madani (2 vols.) by Shaykh Akram al-'Umari [available in English under the title *Madinan Society at the Time of the Prophet (*peace and blessings of Allāh be upon him)]
Siyār A'lām al-Nubalā'
Minhaj Kitābāt al-Tarikh al-Islāmi by Muḥammad ibn Samil al-Salāmī

There are many other good books on various topics, such as those by:

Shaykh Muḥammad ibn 'Abd al-Waḥḥāb
Shaykh 'Abd al-Raḥmān ibn Nāsir al-Sa'di
Shaykh 'Umar Sulaymān al-Ashqar
Shaykh Muḥammad ibn Aḥmad ibn Ismā'il al-Muqaddim
Prof. Muḥammad Muḥammad Husayn
Shaykh Muḥammad Jamil Zayno
Prof. Husayn al-'Awayishah's books on *al-Raqā'iq* (topics to soften the heart and strengthen *īmān*)
Al-Īmān by Muḥammad Na'im Yasin
Al-Walā' wa'l-Barā' by Shaykh Muḥammad Sa'īd al-Qaḥṭānī [available in English translation]
Al-Inhirafāt al-'Aqdiyyah fi'l-Qarnayn al-Thani 'Ashara wa'l-Thalith 'Ashara by 'Alī ibn Bukhayt al-Zahranī
Al-Muslimūn wa Zahirat al-Hazimah al-Nafsiyyah by 'Abd-Allāh al-Shabanah
Al-Mar'ah bayn al-Fiqh wa'l-Qanūn by Mustafa al-Siba'i
Al-Usrah al-Muslimah amam al-video wa'l-tilifiziyūn by Marwān Kijik
Al-Mar'ah al-Muslimah I'dadātuha wa mas'ūliyatuha by Aḥmad Abū Batin

Mas'ūliyāt al-Abb al-Muslim fi Tarbiyāt Walādihi by 'Adnan Baharith
Hijab al-Muslimah by Aḥmad al-Barazi
Wa Ja'a Dawr al-Majūs by 'Abd-Allāh Muḥammad al-Gharib
Books by Shaykh Bakr Abū Zayd
Abhath al-Shaykh Mashūr Hasan Salmān

There are many other useful, good books - what we have mentioned is only by way of example, and is by no means a complete list. There are also many useful pamphlets and booklets, but it would take too long to list everything. The Muslim should consult others and think hard. Whomever Allāh wishes good for, He helps him to understand His religion.

Home audio library

Having a cassette player in every home may be used for good or for evil. How can we use it in a manner that is pleasing to Allāh?

One of the ways in which we can achieve this is to have a home audio library containing good Islāmic tapes by scholars, *fuqahā'*, lecturers, *khātibs* and preachers.

Listening to tapes of Qur'ān recitation by some Imāms, for example those recorded during *Tarāwih* prayers, will have a great impact on family members, whether by impressing upon them the meanings of the Revelation, or by helping them to memorize Qur'ān because of repeated listening. It will also protect them by letting them hear Qur'ānic recitation rather than the music and singing of the *Shayṭān*, because it is not right for the words of *al-Raḥmān* (Allāh) to be mixed with the music of the *Shayṭān* in the heart of the believer.

Tapes of *fatwas* may have a great effect on family members and help them to understand various rulings, which will have an impact on their daily lives. We suggest listening to tapes of *fatwas* given by scholars such as Shaykh 'Abd al-'Azīz ibn Baz, Shaykh Muḥammad Nāsir al-Din al-Albānī, Shaykh Muḥammad Sāliḥ al-'Uthaymin, Shaykh Sālih al-Fawzān, and other trustworthy scholars.

Muslims must also pay attention to the sources from which they take *fatwas*, because this is the matter of religion, so look to where you take your religion from. You should take it from someone who is known to be righteous and pious, who bases his *fatwas* on sound *aḥādīth*, who is not fanatical in his adherence to a *madhhab*, who follows sound evidence and adheres to a middle path without being either extreme or too lenient. Ask an expert.

ٱلرَّحْمَٰنُ فَسْـَٔلْ بِهِۦ خَبِيرًا ﴿٥٩﴾

...Allāh, Most Gracious: ask, then about Him of any acquainted (with such things).

[*al-Furqān* 25:59]

Listening to lectures by those who are striving to raise the awareness of the *ummah,* establish proof and denounce evil, is very important for establishing individual personalities in the Muslim home.

There are many tapes and lectures, and the Muslim needs to know the features of the sound methodology so as to distinguish sound lecturers from others and look for their tapes, which they can listen to with confidence. Among these features are:

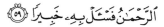

The lecturer should be a believer in the *'Aqīdah* of the Saved Group, *Ahl al-Sunnah wa'l-Jamā'ah*, adhering to the Sunnah and firmly rejecting *bidʿah*. The speaker should be moderate, neither extremist nor lenient.

He should base his talks on sound *aḥādīth*, and beware of weak and fabricated *aḥādīth*.

He should have insight into people's situations and the realities of the *ummah*, and should offer the appropriate remedy for any problem, giving the people what they need.

He should speak the truth as much as he can, and not utter falsehood or please the people by angering Allaah.

We often find that tapes for children have a great influence on them, whether by helping them to memorize Qur'ān by listening to a young reader, or invocations to be recited at various times of day and night, or Islamic manners, or *nashīds* (religious 'songs' with no instrumental accompaniment) with a useful message, and so on.

Putting tapes in drawers in an organized fashion will make it easier to find them, and will also protect them from getting damaged or from being played with by young children. We should distribute good tapes by giving or lending them to others after listening to them. Having a recorder in the kitchen will be very useful for the lady of the house, and having a recorder in the bedroom will help a person make good use of time until the last moments of the day.

Inviting good and righteous people and seekers of knowledge to visit the home.

رَّبِّ ٱغْفِرْ لِى وَلِوَٰلِدَىَّ وَلِمَن دَخَلَ بَيْتِىَ
مُؤْمِنًا وَلِلْمُؤْمِنِينَ وَٱلْمُؤْمِنَٰتِ وَلَا تَزِدِ ٱلظَّٰلِمِينَ إِلَّا تَبَارًۢا ﴿٢٨﴾

My Lord! Forgive me, and my parents, and him who enters my home as a believer, and all the believing men and women...

[*Nūḥ* (71) : 28]

If people of faith enter your home, it will increase in light (*nūr*), and will bring many benefits because of your conversations and discussion with them. The bearer of musk will either give you some, or you will buy from him, or you will find that he has a pleasant scent. When children, brothers and parents sit with such visitors, and women listen from behind a curtain or screen to what is said, this offers an educational experience to all. If you bring good people into your home, by doing so you keep bad people from coming in a wreaking havoc.

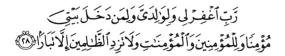

LEARNING THE ISLĀMIC RULINGS WITH REGARD TO HOUSES

These include:

Praying in the house

With regard to men, the Prophet (ﷺ) said:

> "The best of prayer is a man's prayer in his house - apart from the prescribed prayers." [1]

It is obligatory to pray (the five daily prayers) in the *masjid*, except if there is a valid excuse. The Messenger of Allāh (ﷺ) also said:

> "A man's voluntary prayers in his house will bring more reward than his voluntary prayers at other people's places, just as his obligatory prayers with the people are better than his obligatory prayers alone." [2]

---

[1] Reported by al-Bukhārī, *al-Fath*, [no. 731].

[2] Reported by Ibn Abī Shaybah, *Ṣaḥīḥ al-Jāmi'*, [2953].

With regard to women, the deeper inside her home her place of prayer is, the better, because the Prophet (ﷺ) said:

> "The best prayer for women is [that offered] in the furthest part of their houses." [3]

A man should not be led in prayer in his own home, and no one should sit in the place where the master of the house usually sits, except with his permission. The Messenger of Allāh (ﷺ) said:

> "A man should not be led in prayer in his place of authority, and no one should sit in his place in his house, except with his permission." [4]

No one should go forward to lead him in prayer, even if they recite Qur'ān better than he does, in a place that he owns or where he has authority, such as a householder in his home, or an imaam in a *masjid.* Similarly, it is not permitted to sit in the private spot of the head of the master of the house, such as a bed or mattress, etc., except with his permission.

---

3 Reported by al-Tabarānī, *Ṣaḥīḥ al-Jāmi'*, [3311].

4 Reported by al-Tirmidhī, [no. 2772].

Seeking permission to enter

يَٰٓأَيُّهَا ٱلَّذِينَ
ءَامَنُواْ لَا تَدۡخُلُواْ بُيُوتًا غَيۡرَ بُيُوتِكُمۡ حَتَّىٰ تَسۡتَأۡنِسُواْ
وَتُسَلِّمُواْ عَلَىٰٓ أَهۡلِهَاۚ ذَٰلِكُمۡ خَيۡرٞ لَّكُمۡ لَعَلَّكُمۡ تَذَكَّرُونَ ٢٧
فَإِن لَّمۡ تَجِدُواْ فِيهَآ أَحَدٗا فَلَا تَدۡخُلُوهَا حَتَّىٰ يُؤۡذَنَ لَكُمۡۖ وَإِن
قِيلَ لَكُمُ ٱرۡجِعُواْ فَٱرۡجِعُواْۖ هُوَ أَزۡكَىٰ لَكُمۡۚ وَٱللَّهُ بِمَا تَعۡمَلُونَ
عَلِيمٞ ٢٨

O you who believe! Enter not houses other than your own, until you have asked permission and greeted those in them, that is better for you, in order that you may remember. And if you find no one therein, still, enter not until permission has been given. And if you are asked to go back, go back, for it is purer for you. And Allāh is All-Knower of what you do.

[*Nūḥ* (24) : 27-28]

وَأۡتُواْ ٱلۡبُيُوتَ مِنۡ أَبۡوَٰبِهَاۚ

...so enter houses through their proper doors...

[*al-Baqarah* (2) :189]

It is permissible to enter houses that are empty if one has some legitimate business there, such as a house prepared for guests.

لَّيۡسَ عَلَيۡكُمۡ جُنَاحٌ أَن تَدۡخُلُواْ بُيُوتًا غَيۡرَ مَسۡكُونَةٖ
فِيهَا مَتَٰعٞ لَّكُمۡۚ وَٱللَّهُ يَعۡلَمُ مَا تُبۡدُونَ وَمَا تَكۡتُمُونَ ٢٩

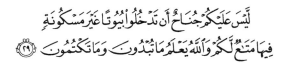

There is no sin on you that you enter (without taking permission) houses uninhabited (i.e., not possessed by anybody), (when) you have any interest in them. And Allāh has knowledge of what you reveal and what you conceal.

[*Nūḥ* (24) : 29]

Not feeling too shy to eat in the houses of friends and relatives, and in houses of friends and relatives and others to which one has the keys, if they have no objection to that.

لَّيْسَ عَلَى ٱلْأَعْمَىٰ حَرَجٌ وَلَا عَلَى ٱلْأَعْرَجِ
حَرَجٌ وَلَا عَلَى ٱلْمَرِيضِ حَرَجٌ وَلَا عَلَىٰٓ أَنفُسِكُمْ أَن تَأْكُلُوا۟
مِنۢ بُيُوتِكُمْ أَوْ بُيُوتِ ءَابَآئِكُمْ أَوْ بُيُوتِ أُمَّهَٰتِكُمْ
أَوْ بُيُوتِ إِخْوَٰنِكُمْ أَوْ بُيُوتِ أَخَوَٰتِكُمْ أَوْ بُيُوتِ
أَعْمَٰمِكُمْ أَوْ بُيُوتِ عَمَّٰتِكُمْ أَوْ بُيُوتِ أَخْوَٰلِكُمْ
أَوْ بُيُوتِ خَٰلَٰتِكُمْ أَوْ مَا مَلَكْتُم مَّفَاتِحَهُۥٓ
أَوْ صَدِيقِكُمْ ۚ لَيْسَ عَلَيْكُمْ جُنَاحٌ أَن تَأْكُلُوا۟
جَمِيعًا أَوْ أَشْتَاتًا ۚ

There is no restriction on the blind, nor any restriction on the lame, nor any restriction on the sick, nor on yourselves, if you eat from your houses, or the houses of your fathers, or the houses of your mothers, or the houses of your brothers, or the houses of your sisters, or the houses of your father's brothers, or the houses of your father's sisters, or the houses of your mother's brothers, or the houses of your mother's sisters, or (from that) whereof you hold keys, or

(from the house) of a friend. No sin on you whether you eat together or apart...

[*Nūḥ* (24) : 61]

Telling children and servants not to barge in to the parent's bedroom without permission at the times when people usually sleep, i.e., before *Fajr*, at siesta time and after *'Isha'*, lest they see something inappropriate. If they see something accidentally at other times, this is forgivable, because they are *tawwāfin* (those who go about in the house) and it is difficult to stop them. Allāh says:

يَٰٓأَيُّهَا ٱلَّذِينَ ءَامَنُوا۟
لِيَسْتَـْٔذِنكُمُ ٱلَّذِينَ مَلَكَتْ أَيْمَٰنُكُمْ وَٱلَّذِينَ لَمْ يَبْلُغُوا۟ ٱلْحُلُمَ مِنكُمْ
ثَلَٰثَ مَرَّٰتٍ ۚ مِّن قَبْلِ صَلَوٰةِ ٱلْفَجْرِ وَحِينَ تَضَعُونَ ثِيَابَكُم مِّنَ ٱلظَّهِيرَةِ
وَمِنۢ بَعْدِ صَلَوٰةِ ٱلْعِشَآءِ ۚ ثَلَٰثُ عَوْرَٰتٍ لَّكُمْ ۚ لَيْسَ عَلَيْكُمْ
وَلَا عَلَيْهِمْ جُنَاحٌۢ بَعْدَهُنَّ ۚ طَوَّٰفُونَ عَلَيْكُم بَعْضُكُمْ عَلَىٰ
بَعْضٍ ۚ كَذَٰلِكَ يُبَيِّنُ ٱللَّهُ لَكُمُ ٱلْءَايَٰتِ ۗ وَٱللَّهُ عَلِيمٌ حَكِيمٌ ﴿٥٨﴾

O you who believe! Let your legal slaves and slave-girls, and those among you who have not come to the age of puberty ask your permission (before they come to your presence) on three occasions: before *Fajr* prayer, and while you put off your clothes for the noonday (rest), and after the *'Isha'* prayer. (These) three times are of privacy for you; other than these times there is no sin on you or on them to move about, - attending (helping) you each other. Thus Allāh makes clear the *āyāt* (verses of this Qurʾaan, showing proofs for the legal aspects of permission for visits, etc.) to

you. And Allāh is All-Knowing, All-Wise.

[*Nūḥ* (24) : 58].

It is forbidden to look into the houses of other people without their permission. The Messenger of Allāh (ﷺ) said:

> "Whoever looks into someone's house without their permission, put his eyes out, and there is no *diyah* or *qisās* [blood money or retaliation] in this case." [5]

A woman who has been divorced by *Ṭalāq* for a first or second time [and could still go back to her husband] should not leave or be made to leave her home during the *ʿiddah*, and she should still be supported financially. Allāh says:

يَٰٓأَيُّهَا ٱلنَّبِيُّ إِذَا طَلَّقۡتُمُ ٱلنِّسَآءَ فَطَلِّقُوهُنَّ لِعِدَّتِهِنَّ وَأَحۡصُواْ
ٱلۡعِدَّةَۖ وَٱتَّقُواْ ٱللَّهَ رَبَّكُمۡۖ لَا تُخۡرِجُوهُنَّ مِنۢ بُيُوتِهِنَّ
وَلَا يَخۡرُجۡنَ إِلَّآ أَن يَأۡتِينَ بِفَٰحِشَةٖ مُّبَيِّنَةٖۚ وَتِلۡكَ حُدُودُ
ٱللَّهِۚ وَمَن يَتَعَدَّ حُدُودَ ٱللَّهِ فَقَدۡ ظَلَمَ نَفۡسَهُۥۚ لَا تَدۡرِي لَعَلَّ
ٱللَّهَ يُحۡدِثُ بَعۡدَ ذَٰلِكَ أَمۡرٗا ١

O Prophet! When you divorce women, divorce them at their *ʿiddah* (prescribed periods), and count (accurately) their *ʿiddah* (periods). And fear Allāh your Lord (O Muslims), and turn them not out of their (husbands) homes, nor shall they (themselves) leave, except in case they are guilty of some open illegal sexual intercourse. And those are the set limits of Allāh. And whoever transgresses the set limits of Allāh, then indeed

---

5 Reported by Aḥmad, *al-Musnad*, [2/385]; *Ṣaḥīḥ al-Jāmiʿ*, [6046].

he has wronged himself. You (the one who divorces his wife) know not, it may be that Allāh will afterward bring some new thing to pass (i.e., to return her back to you, if this as the first or second divorce).

[*al-Ṭalāq* (65) : 1]

It is permissible for a man to forsake his rebellious wife inside or outside the home, according to the interests prescribed by *sharīʾah* in any given case. The evidence for forsaking her inside the home is the *ayāh*:

وَٱهْجُرُوهُنَّ فِى ٱلْمَضَاجِعِ

...refuse to share their beds...

[*al-Nisāʾ* (4) : 34]

With regard to forsaking women outside the home, this is what happened when the Messenger of Allāh (ﷺ) forsook his wives, leaving them in their apartments and staying in a room outside the houses of his wives. [6]

One should not stay alone overnight in the house. Ibn ʿUmar (may Allāh be pleased with him) reported that the Prophet (ﷺ) forbade being alone and said that a man should not stay overnight alone or travel alone. [7]

This is because of the feelings of loneliness etc., that come from being alone, and also because of the possibility of attacks by enemies or robbers, or the possibility of sickness. If one has

6 Reported by al-Bukhārī.

7 Reported by Aḥmad in *al-Musnad*, [2/91].

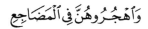

a companion, he can help fight off attacks, and can help if one gets sick.[8]

Not sleeping on the roof of a house that has no protecting wall, lest one fall. The Messenger of Allāh (ﷺ) said:

> "Whoever sleeps on the roof of a house that has no protecting wall, nobody is responsible for what happens to him." [9]

This is because one who is asleep may roll over in his sleep, and if there is no wall he may fall off the roof and be killed. In such a case, nobody would be to blame for his death; or his negligence would cause Allāh to lift His protection from him, because he did not take the necessary precautions. The *ḥadīth* may mean either.

Pet cats do not make vessels *nājis* (impure) if they drink from them, or make food *nājis* if they eat from it. ʿAbd-Allāh ibn Abī Qatādah reported from his father that water was put out for him to make *wuḍū'* , and a cat came and lapped at the water. He took the water and did *wuḍū'* with it, and they said,

> "O Abū Qatādah! The cat drank from it. He said, I heard the Messenger of Allāh (ﷺ) say: 'Cats are part of the household, and they are among those who go around in your houses.'" [10]

---

[8] See *al-Fath al-Rabbānī*, [5/64].

[9] Reported by Abū Dāwūd, *al-Sunan*, [no. 5041]; *Ṣaḥīḥ al-Jāmi'*, [6113]; its commentary is in *'Awn al-Maʿbūd*, [13/384].

[10] Reported by Aḥmad in *al-Musnad*, [5/309]; *Ṣaḥīḥ al-Jāmi'*, [3694].

According to another report he said:

> "They [cats] are not *nājis*; they are among those who go around [*al-tawwāfīn wa'l-tawwāfāt* - refers to children, servants, etc.] in your houses." [11]

Knowing the advantages of *khushū'* in *Ṣalāh*

These include:

The Prophet (ﷺ) said:

> "There is no Muslim man who, when the time for a prescribed prayer comes, he does *wuḍū'* properly, has the proper attitude of *khushū'* , and bows properly, but it will be an expiation for all his previous sins, so long as they were not major sins (*kabīrah*). And this is the case for life." [12]

The reward recorded is in proportion to the degree of *khushū'*, as the Prophet (ﷺ) said:

> "A slave may pray and have nothing recorded for it except a tenth of it, or a ninth, or an eighth, or a seventh, or a sixth, or a fifth, or a quarter, or a third, or a half." [13]

---

[11] Reported by Aḥmad in *al-Musnad*, [5/309]; *Ṣaḥīḥ al-Jāmi'*, [2437].

[12] Reported by Muslim, [1/206, no. 7/4/2].

[13] Reported by Imām Aḥmad; *Ṣaḥīḥ al-Jāmi'*, [1626].

Only the parts of his prayer where he focused and concentrated properly will be of any avail to him. It was reported that Ibn 'Abbās (may Allāh be pleased with him) said: 'You will only have from your prayer that which you focused on.' Sins will be forgiven if you concentrate properly and have full *khushū'*, as the Prophet (ﷺ) said:

> "When a slave stands and prays, all his sins are brought and placed on his head and shoulders. Every time he bows or prostrates, some of them fall from him." [14]

al-Manāwī said:

> 'What is meant is that every time a pillar (essential part) of the prayer is completed, part of his sins fall from him, until when he finishes his prayer, all his sins will be removed. This is in a prayer where all the conditions are met and the essential parts are complete. What we understand from the words 'slave' and 'stands' is that he is standing before the King of Kings [Allāh] in the position of a humble slave.'[15]

The one who prays with *khushū'* will feel lighter when he finishes his prayer, as if his burdens have been lifted from him. He will feel at ease and refreshed, so that he will wish he had not stopped praying, because it is such a source of joy and comfort for him in this world. He will keep feeling that he is in a constricting prison until he starts to pray again; he will find comfort in prayer instead of wanting just to get it over and done with.

---

14 Reported by al-Bayhaqī in *al-Sunan al-Kubrā*, [3/10]; see also *Ṣaḥīḥ al-Jāmi'*.

15 Reported by al-Bayhaqī in *al-Sunan al-Kubrā*, [3/10]; see also *Ṣaḥīḥ al-Jāmi'*.

Those who love prayer say: we pray and find comfort in our prayer, just as their leader, example and Prophet (ﷺ) said,

> "O Bilāl, let us find comfort in prayer. He did not say; 'Let us get it over and done with.'"

The Prophet (ﷺ) said,

> "My joy has been made in prayer."

So whoever finds his joy in prayer, how can he bear to look for joy anywhere else, or to keep away from it?[16]

Striving to offer invocations at the appropriate times during the prayer, especially in *sujūd*

There is no doubt that talking to Allāh, humbling oneself before Him, asking things from Him and earnestly seeking His help, all help to strengthen the slave's ties to his Lord and increase his *khushū'*. Invocation is an act of worship, and we are commanded to make invocation. Allāh says:

تَدۡعُونَهُۥ تَضَرُّعٗا وَخُفۡيَةٗ

...call upon Him in humility and in secret...

[*al-An'ām* (6) : 63].

The Prophet (ﷺ) said:

[16] *Al-Wābil al-Sayib*, [p.37].

> "Whoever does not call on Allāh, Allāh will be angry with him." [17]

It was reported that the Prophet (ﷺ) used to make *duʿā* at specific places in the prayer, i.e., in *sujūd*, between the two prostrations and after the *Tashahhud*. The greatest of these is in *sujūd*, because the Prophet (ﷺ) said,

> "The closest that the slave can be to his Lord is when he is prostrating, so increase your *duʿā* [at that time]."[18]

And he said:

> "...as for *sujūd*, strive hard to make *duʿā* in it, for it is bound to be answered for you." [19]

One of the *duʿā's* which the Prophet (ﷺ) used to recite in his *sujūd* was:

«اللَّهُمَّ اغْفِرْ لِي ذَنْبِي كُلَّهُ، دِقَّهُ وجِلَّهُ، وَأَوَّلَهُ وَآخِرَهُ وَعَلَانِيَتَهُ وَسِرَّهُ»

"Allāhumma' ghfir li dhanbī diqqahu wa jillahu wa awwalahu wa ākhirahu wa 'alāniyatahu wa sirrahu."

"O Allāh, forgive me my sins, the minor and the major, the first and the last, the open and the

---

[17] Reported by al-Tirmidhī, *Kitāb al-Da'wāt*, [1/426]; classed as ḥasan in *Ṣaḥīḥ al-Tirmidhī*, [2686].

[18] Reported by Muslim, *Kitāb al-Ṣalāh, Bāb mā yuqālu fi'l-rukū' wa'l-sujūd*. [No. 215].

[19] Reported by Muslim, *Kitāb al-Ṣalāh, Bāb al-Nahy 'an qirā'at al-Qur'ān fi'l-rukū' wa'l-sujūd*, [no. 207].

hidden."[20]

He (ﷺ) also used to say,

«اللَّهُمَّ اغْفِرْ لِي مَا أَسْرَرْتُ، وَمَا أَعْلَنْتُ

"Allāhumma'ghfir lī mā asrartu wa mā a'lantu."

"O Allāh, forgive me what I have done in secret and done openly."[21]

We have already described some of the *du'ā's* that he used to recite between the two *sajdahs*.

One of the things that he (ﷺ) used to recite after the *Tashahhud* is what we learn from the *ḥadīth*:

> "When any one of you finishes the *Tashahhud*, let him seek refuge with Allāh from four things, from the punishment of Hell, from the punishment of the grave, from the trials (*fitnah*) of life and death, and from the evil of the *Dajjāl* (Antichrist)."

He used to say,

اَللّهُمَّ إِنِّي أَعُوذُ بِكَ مِنْ شَرِّ مَا عَمِلْتُ، وَمِنْ شَرِّ مَا لَمْ أَعْمَلْ

"Allāhumma innī a'ūdhu bika min sharri mā 'amiltu wa min sharri mā lam a'mal."

---

[20] Reported by Muslim, *Kitāb al-Ṣalāh, Bāb mā yuqālu fi'l-rukū' wa'l-sujūd*, [no. 216].

[21] Reported by al-Nisā'i, *al-Mujtabā*, [2/569]; *Ṣaḥīḥ al-Jāmi'*, [1067].

"O Allāh, I seek refuge with You from the evil of what I have done and the evil of what I have not done."

اَللّهُمَّ حَاسِبْنِي حِسَاباً يَسِيراً

"Allāhumma hāsibnī hisābān yasīran."

"O Allāh, make my accounting easy."

He taught Abū Bakr al-Ṣiddīq (may Allāh be pleased with him) to say,

«اللَّهُمَّ إِنِّي ظَلَمْتُ نَفْسِي ظُلْمًا كَثِيرًا، وَلَا يَغْفِرُ الذُّنُوبَ إِلَّا أَنْتَ، فَاغْفِرْ لِي مَغْفِرَةً مِنْ عِنْدِكَ وَارْحَمْنِي إِنَّكَ أَنْتَ الْغَفُورُ الرَّحِيمُ»

"Allāhumma innī ẓalamtu nafsī ẓulmān kathīrān, wa lā yaghfir al-dhunūba illā anta, faghfir lī maghfiratan min 'indaka wārḥamnī innaka anta al-Ghafūr al-Raḥīm."

"O Allāh, I have wronged myself very much, and no one can forgive sin but You. Grant me forgiveness from You and have mercy on me, for You are the All-Forgiving, Most Merciful."

He heard a man saying in his *Tashahhud*:

«اللَّهُمَّ إِنِّي أَسْأَلُكَ يَا اللهُ بِأَنَّكَ الْوَاحِدُ الأَحَدُ الصَّمَدُ الَّذِي لَمْ يَلِدْ وَلَمْ يُولَدْ وَلَمْ يَكُنْ لَهُ كُفُواً أَحَدٌ، أَنْ تَغْفِرَ لِي ذُنُوبِي إِنَّكَ أَنْتَ الْغَفُورُ الرَّحِيمُ»

> "Allāhumma innī as'aluka yā Allāh al-Aḥad al-Samad alladhī lam yalid wa lam yūlad wa lam yakum lahu kufuwan aḥad an taghfir lī dhunūbī innaka anta'l-Ghafūr al-Raḥīm."
>
> "O Allāh, I ask You O Allāh, the One, the Self-Sufficient Master, Who begets not neither is begotten, and there is none like unto Him, to forgive me my sins, for You are the All-Forgiving, Most Merciful."

He (ﷺ) said to his companions: 'He has been forgiven, he has been forgiven.'

He heard another man saying,

«اللَّهُمَّ إِنِّي أَسْأَلُكَ بِأَنَّ لَكَ الْحَمْدَ لَا إِلٰهَ إِلَّا أَنْتَ وَحْدَكَ لَا شَرِيكَ
لَكَ، الْمَنَّانُ، يَابَدِيعَ السَّمٰوَاتِ وَالأَرْضِ يَا ذَا الْجَلَالِ وَالإِكْرَامِ، يَاحَيُّ
يَاقَيُّومُ إِنِّي أَسْأَلُكَ الْجَنَّةَ وَأَعُوذُ بِكَ مِنَ النَّارِ»

> "Allāhumma innī as'aluka bi-anna laka'l-ḥamd, lā ilāha ill anta waḥdaka lā sharīka lak al-Mannān yā badī' al-samawāti wa'l-ard, yā dhā'l-jalāli wa'l-ikrām, ya ḥayyu yaa qayyūm, innī as'aluka al-jannah wa a'ūdhu bika min al-nār."
>
> "O Allāh, I ask You as all praise is due to You, there is no god but You Alone, with no partner or associate, the Bestower, O Originator of the heavens and earth, O Possessor of Glory and Honour, O Ever-Living, O Self-Sustaining, I ask You for Paradise and I seek refuge with You from Hell."

The Prophet (ﷺ) said to his companions:

> "'Do you know by what did he ask Allāh?' They said; 'Allāh and His Messenger know best.'"

He said,

> "By the One in Whose hand is my soul, he asked Allāh by His greatest Name (*ismuhu'l-a'ẓam*) which, when He is called by it, He responds, and if He is asked by it, He gives."

The last thing he would say between the *Tashahhud* and the *Taslīm* was:

«اللَّهُمَّ اغْفِرْ لِي مَا قَدَّمْتُ، وَمَا أَخَّرْتُ، وَمَا أَسْرَرْتُ، وَمَا أَعْلَنْتُ، وَمَا أَسْرَفْتُ، وَمَا أَنْتَ أَعْلَمُ بِهِ مِنِّي. أَنْتَ الْمُقَدِّمُ، وَأَنْتَ الْمُؤَخِّرُ لَا إِلَـهَ إِلَّا أَنْتَ»

> "Allāhumma'aghfir lī mā qaddamtu wa ma akhkhartu wa mā asrartu wa mā a'lantu wa mā asraftu wa mā anta aṛlam bihi minnī antaṛl-muqaddim wa anta'l-mu'akhkhir, laa ilāha illā anta."

> "O Allāh, forgive me what I have done in the past, and what I will do in the future, and what I have concealed, and what I have done openly, and what I have exceeded in, whatever You know about more than I. You are the Bringer-Forward, and You are the Delayer, there is no god except You." [22]

[22] These *du'ā's* and others, along with their isnāds, are to be found in *Sifāt al-Salāh* by al-'Allāmah al-Albānī, [p.163].

Memorizing *du'ā's* like these will solve the problem that some people have of remaining silent behind the *imām* when they have finished the *Tashahhud* because they do not know what they should say.

Adhkār to be recited after prayer

These also help to strengthen *khushū'* in the heart and reinforce the blessings and benefits of the prayer.

Without a doubt, one of the best ways of preserving and protecting a good action is to follow it up with another. So the one who thinks about the *adhkār* that come after the prayer will find that they begin with seeking forgiveness three times, as if the worshipper is seeking forgiveness from his Lord for any shortcomings that may have occurred in his prayer or his *khushū'*. It is also important to pay attention to *nāfil* (supererogatory) prayers, because they make up for anything lacking in the *farḍ* (obligatory) prayers, including any failure with regard to *khushū'*.

Having discussed things that help us to have *khushū'* we now move on to a discussion of meetings at home.

MEETINGS AT HOME

Removing anything that may distract the worshipper

Anas (may Allāh be pleased with him) said: "Ā'ishah had a decorated, colourful curtain which she used to cover the side of her house. The Prophet (ﷺ) said to her,

> "Take it away from me, because its decorations keep distracting me when I pray."' [1]

al-Qāsim reported that 'Ā'ishah (may Allāh be pleased with her) had a cloth with decorations on it, which she used to cover a small sunken alcove (used for sleeping or storage). The Prophet (ﷺ) used to pray facing it, and he said,

> "Take it away from me, because its decorations keep distracting me when I pray. So she took it away and made pillows out of it." [2]

Another indication of this is the fact that when the Prophet

---

[1] Reported by al-Bukhārī, *Fath al-Bārī*, [10/391].

(ﷺ) entered the *Ka'bah* to pray in it, he saw two ram's horns. When he had prayed, he told 'Uthmān al-Hajabī,

> "I forgot to tell you to cover the horns, because there should not be anything in the House to distract the worshipper." [3]

This also includes avoiding praying in places where people pass through, or where there is a lot of noise and voices of people talking, or where they are engaging in conversations, arguments etc., or where there are visual distractions.

One should also avoid praying in places that are very hot or very cold, if possible. The Prophet (ﷺ) told us to delay praying *Zuḥr* in summer until the hottest part of the day was over.

Ibn al-Qayyim (may Allāh have mercy on him) said:

> "Praying when it is intensely hot prevents a person from having the proper *khushū'* and presence of mind, and he does his worship reluctantly, so the Prophet wisely told them to delay praying until the heat had lessened somewhat, so that they could pray with presence of mind and thus achieve the purpose of prayer, i.e., having *khushū'* and turning to Allāh." [4]

---

[2] Reported by Muslim in his *Ṣaḥīḥ*, [3/1668].

[3] Reported by Abū Dāwūd, 2030; *Ṣaḥīḥ al-Jāmi'*, [2504].

[4] *Al-Wābil al-Sayib*, Dār al-Bayān edn., [p.22].

Not praying in a garment that has decorations, writing, bright colours or pictures that will distract the worshipper

'Ā'ishah (may Allāh be pleased with her) said:

> 'The Prophet (ﷺ) stood up to pray wearing a checkered shirt, and he looked at the patterns in it. When he had finished his prayer, he said, "Take this shirt to Abū Jaham ibn Ḥudhayfah and bring me an *anbajānī* (a garment with no decorations or checks), because it distracted me when I was praying."'

According to another report:

> "These checks distracted me."

According to another report:

> "He had a checkered shirt, which used to distract him whilst he was praying." [5]

It is better not to pray in a garment that has pictures on it, and we should be especially careful to avoid garments with pictures of animate beings, like many garments that are widely available nowadays.

---

[5] Reports in *Ṣaḥīḥ Muslim*, [no. 556, part 3/391].

Not praying when there is food prepared that one wants to eat

The Messenger of Allāh (ﷺ) said:

"Do not pray when there is food prepared." [6]

If food has been prepared and served, or if it is offered, a person should eat first, because he will not be able to concentrate properly and have *khushū'* if he leaves it and gets up to pray when he is wanting to eat. He should not even hasten to finish eating, because the Prophet (ﷺ) said:

> "If the dinner is served and the time for prayer comes, eat dinner before praying *Ṣalāt al-Maghrib*, and do not rush to finish your meal."

According to another report:

> "If dinner has been put out and the *iqāmah* has been given for prayer, eat dinner first and do not rush to finish it." [7]

[6] Reported by Muslim, no. 560).

[7] Agreed upon, al-Bukhārī, *Kitāb al-Āẓān, Bāb idhā hadara al-ta'āmu wa uqīmat al-Ṣalāh*; Muslim, [no. 557-559].

Not praying when one needs to answer the call of nature

No doubt one of the things that can prevent proper *khushū'* is praying when one needs to go to the washroom. The Prophet (ﷺ) forbade praying when one is suppressing the urge to urinate or defecate.[8]

If anyone is in this position, he should first go to the bathroom and answer the call of nature, even if he misses whatever he misses of the congregational prayer, because the Prophet (ﷺ) said,

> "If any one of you needs to go to the toilet, and the prayer has begun, he should go to the toilet first." [9]

If this happens to a person whilst he is praying, he should stop praying, go and answer the call of nature, purify himself then pray, because the Prophet (ﷺ) said,

> "There is no prayer when there is food prepared or if one is suppressing the urge to expel waste matter." [10]

Without a doubt, this trying to suppress the urge takes away *khushū'*. This ruling also applies to suppressing the urge to pass wind.

---

8 Reported by Ibn Mājah in his *Sunan*, [no. 617;] *Ṣaḥīḥ al-Jāmi'*, [no. 6832].

9 Reported by Abū Dāwūd, [no. 88]; *Ṣaḥīḥ al-Jāmi'*, [no. 299].

10 Reported by Muslim, [no. 560].

Not praying when one feels sleepy

Anas ibn Mālik said, 'The Messenger of Allāh (ﷺ) said:

> "If any one of you feels sleepy when he is praying, he should sleep until he [is rested enough to] know what he is saying, i.e., he should take a nap until he no longer feels drowsy..."' [11]

This may happen when one is praying *qiyām al-layl*, at the time when prayers are answered, and a person may pray against himself without realizing it. This *ḥadīth* also includes fard prayers, when a person is confident that he will still have enough time to pray after taking a nap.[12]

Not praying behind someone who is talking (or sleeping)

The Prophet (ﷺ) forbade this; he said:

> "Do not pray behind one who is sleeping or one who is talking." [13]

Because one who is talking will distract the worshipper with his talk, and one who is sleeping may expose something that will

---

[11] Reported by al-Bukhārī, [no. 210].

[12] *Fath al-Bārī, Sharḥ Kitāb al-Wuḍū', Bāb al-wuḍū' min al-nawm.*

[13] Reported by Abū Dāwūd, [no. 694]; *Ṣaḥīḥ al-Jāmi'*, [no. 375]. He said, a *ḥasan ḥadīth.*

distract the worshipper.

Al-Khaṭṭābī (may Allāh have mercy on him) said:

> 'As for praying behind people who are talking, al-Shāfa'i and Aḥmad ibn Ḥanbal considered this to be *makrūh*, because their talk distracts the worshipper from his prayer.' [14]

As regards not praying behind someone who is sleeping, a number of scholars thought that the evidence for this was weak.[15]

al-Bukhārī, may Allāh have mercy on him, quoted the *ḥadīth* of 'Ā'ishah in his *Ṣaḥīḥ, Bāb al-Ṣalāh khalf al-Nā'im*:

> "The Prophet (ﷺ) used to pray whilst I was lying across from him on his bed..." [16]

Mujāhid, Tāwūs and Mālik thought it *makrūh* to pray facing someone who was sleeping, lest he expose something that would distract the worshipper from his prayer. [17]

If there is no risk of that happening, then it is not *makrūh* to pray behind someone who is sleeping. And Allāh knows best.

---

14 *'Awn al-Ma'būd*, 2/388).

15 Including Abū Dāwūd in his *Sunan, Kitāb al-Ṣalāh, Tafrīr Abwāb al-Witr, Bāb al-Du'ā*, and Ibn Hajr in *Fath al-Bārī, Sharḥ Bāb al-Ṣalāh khalf al-Nā'im, Kitāb al-Ṣalāh.*

16 Reported by al-Bukhārī, *Kitāb al-Ṣalāh.*

17 *Fath al-Bārī*, ibid.

Not occupying oneself with smoothing the ground in front of one

al-Bukhārī reported from Mu'ayqīb (may Allāh be pleased with him) that the Prophet (ﷺ) said concerning a man's smoothing the ground when he prostrates,

"If you have to do that, then do it only once." [18]

The Messenger of Allāh (ﷺ) said:

"Do not wipe (the ground) when you are praying, but if you have to, then do it only once." [19]

The reason for this prohibition is so as to maintain *khushū'*, and so that a person will not make too many extra movements in prayer. If the place where one is going to prostrate needs to be smoothed, it is better to do this before starting to pray.

This also applies to wiping the forehead or nose when praying. The Prophet (ﷺ) used to prostrate in water and mud, which would leave traces on his forehead, but he did not bother to wipe it off every time he raised his head from *sujūd*. It remained there because he was so deeply absorbed in his prayer and his *khushū'* was so strong that he took not notice of it. The Prophet (ﷺ) said:

"Prayer is an occupation in itself." [20]

---

[18] *Fath al-Bārī*, [3/79].

[19] Reported by Abū Dāwūd, [no. 946]; *Ṣaḥīḥ al-Jāmi'*, [no. 7452].

[20] Reported by al-Bukhārī, *Fath al-Bārī*, [3/72].

Ibn Abī Shaybah reported that Abu'l-Dardā' said:

> 'Even if I were to get red camels, I would not like to wipe the gravel from my forehead.'

ḫĪyād said:

> 'The *salaf* did not like to wipe their foreheads before they finished praying.' [21]

Just as a worshipper should avoid anything that will distract him from his prayer, by the same token he should avoid disturbing others. This includes:

Not disturbing others with one's recitation

The Messenger of Allāh (ﷺ) said:

> "All of you are speaking to your Lord, so do not disturb one another, and do not raise your voices above one another when reciting" or he said, "in prayer." [22]

According to another report, he (ﷺ)said,

> "Do not compete with one another in raising your voices when reciting Qur'ān." [23]

---

21 *al-Fath*, [3/79].

22 Reported by Abū Dāwūd, [2/83]; *Ṣaḥīḥ al-Jāmi'*, [no. 752].

23 Reported by Imām Aḥmad, [2/36]; *Ṣaḥīḥ al-Jāmi'*, [1951].

Not turning around during prayer

Abū Dharr (may Allāh be pleased with him) said: 'The Messenger of Allāh (ﷺ) said:

> "Allāh continues to turn towards His slave whilst he is praying, so long as he does not turn away, but if he turns away, [Allāh] turns away from him."' [24]

Turning away during prayer is of two types:

i. The turning away of the heart to something other than Allāh.
ii. The turning away of the eyes.

Both of them are not allowed, and are detrimental to the reward for the prayer. The Messenger of Allāh (ﷺ) was asked about turning away during prayer, and he said:

> "It is something that *Shayṭān* steals from a person's prayer." [25]

The one who turns away with his heart or his eyes during prayer is like a man who is called by the ruler and made to stand before him, and when the ruler starts to address him, he turns away, looking to the right and the left, not listening to what the ruler is saying and not understanding a word of it, because his heart and mind are elsewhere. What does this man think the ruler will do

---

[24] Reported by Abū Dāwūd, [no. 909]; *Ṣaḥīḥ Abī Dāwūd.*

[25] Reported by al-Bukhārī, *Kitāb al-Āẓān*, *Bāb al-Iltifāt fi'l-Ṣalāh.*

to him?

The least that he deserves is that when he leaves the ruler, he is hated and no longer valued. One who prays like this is not equal to one who prays with the proper presence of mind, turning to Allāh in his prayer in such a way that he feels the greatness of the One before Whom he is standing, and he is filled with fear and submission; he feels too shy before his Lord to turn to anyone else or to turn away. The difference between their prayers is as Ḥassān ibn ʿAtiyah said:

> 'The two men may be in one congregation, but the difference in virtue between them is as great as the distance between heaven and earth. One of them is turning with all his heart towards Allāh, whilst the other is negligent and forgetful.' [26]

As for turning away for a genuine reason, this is permissble. Abū Dāwūd reported that Saḥl ibn al-Ḥanzaliyyah said:

> 'We started praying - *Ṣalāt al-Subḥ* (*Fajr*) - and the Messenger of Allāh (ﷺ) was looking at the ravine.'

Abū Dāwūd said:

> 'He had sent a horseman at night to guard the ravine.' This is like when he carried Umāmah bint Abi'l-ʿĀs, and when he opened the door for ʿĀ'ishah, and when he came down from the minbar whilst praying in order to teach them, and when he stepped back during *Ṣalāt al-Kusūf* (prayer at the time of an eclipse),

---

[26] *Al-Wābil al-Sayib* by Ibn al-Qayyim, Dār al-Bayān, [p. 36].

and when he grabbed and strangled the *Shayṭān* when he wanted to interrupt his prayer. He also ordered that snakes and scorpions should be killed even during prayer, and a person who is praying should stop and even fight one who wants to pass in front of him whilst he is praying. He told women to clap during prayer [if they spot a mistake on the part of the *imām*], and he used to wave or gesture to people who greeted him whilst he was praying. These and other actions may be done in cases of necessity, but if there is no necessity, then they are just idle gestures that cancel out *khushū'* and are therefore not allowed during prayer." [27]

Not raising one's gaze to the heavens

The Prophet (ﷺ) forbade us to do this and issued a warning against it. He said:

> "When any one of you is praying, he should not lift his gaze to the heavens, lest he lose his sight." [28]

According to another report, he (ﷺ) said:

> "What is wrong with people who lift their gaze to the heavens whilst they are praying?"

According to another report, he (ﷺ) said:

---

[27] *Majmū' al-Fatāwa*, [22/559].

[28] Reported by Imām Aḥmad, [5/294]; *Ṣaḥīḥ al-Jāmi'*, [no. 762].

> "that they raise their gaze when they make *du'ā* during *ṣalāh*?" [29]

He spoke out strongly against it, to the extent that he (ﷺ) said,

> "Let them stop it, or their eyesight will be taken away." [30]

Not spitting in front of one when praying

This is incompatible with *khushū'* and good manners before Allāh. The Prophet (ﷺ) said:

> "When any one of you is praying, let him not spit in front of himself, for Allāh is before him when he prays." [31]

He also (ﷺ) said:

> "When any one of you stands up to pray, he should not spit in front of himself, because he is talking to Allāh - may He be blessed and exalted - as long as he is in his prayer place; and he should not [spit] to his right, because there is an angel on his right. He should spit to his left, or beneath his feet, and bury it." [32]

---

29 Reported by Muslim, [no. 429].

30 Reported by Imām Aḥmad, [5/258]; *Ṣaḥīḥ al-Jāmi'*, [5574].

31 Reported by al-Bukhārī in his *Ṣaḥīḥ*, [no. 397].

32 Reported by al-Bukhārī, *al-Fath*, [no. 416, 1/512].

He (ﷺ) said:

> "When one of you stands to pray, he is talking to his Lord, and his Lord is between him and the *qiblah*, so none of you should spit in the direction of his *qiblah*, but to his left or under his feet." [33]

If the mosque is furnished with carpets and so on, as is the norm nowadays, if a person needs to spit, he can take out a handkerchief or whatever, spit into it, and put it away again.

Trying not to yawn when praying

The Messenger of Allāh (ﷺ) said:

> "If any one of you feels the urge to yawn during prayer, let him suppress it as much as he can, lest the *Shayṭān* enter..." [34]

If the *Shayṭān* enters, he will be more able to disturb the worshipper's *khushū'*, in addition to laughing at him when he yawns.

---

[33] Reported by al-Bukhārī, *al-Fath al-Bārī*, [no. 417, 1/513].

[34] Reported by Muslim, [4/2293].

Not putting one's hands on one's hips when praying

Abū Hurayrah said:

> "The Messenger of Allāh (ﷺ) forbade putting the hands on the hips during prayer." [35]

Ziyād ibn Subayh al-Hanafī said:

> 'I prayed beside Ibn 'Umar and I put my hand on my hip, but he struck my hand. When he had finished praying, he said, "This is crossing in prayer. The Messenger of Allāh (ﷺ) used to forbid this."' [36]

It was reported that the Prophet (ﷺ) said that this posture is how the people of Hell rest; we seek refuge with Allāh from that.[37]

---

[35] Reported by Abū Dāwūd [no. 947]; *Ṣaḥīḥ al-Bukhārī, Kitāb al-'Aml fi'l-Ṣalāh, Bāb al-Hadhr fi'l-Ṣalāh.*

[36] Reported by Imām Aḥmad, [2/106] and others. Classed as ṣaḥīḥ by al-Ḥāfiẓ al-'Irāqi in *Takhrīj al-Ihyā'*. See *al-Irwā'*, [2/94].

[37] Reported by al-Bayhaqī from Abū Hurayrah. Al-'Irāqi said, its *isnād* appears to be *ṣaḥīḥ*.

Not letting one's clothes hang down (*saḍl*) during prayer

It was reported that the Messenger of Allāh (ﷺ) forbade letting one's clothes hang down during prayer or for a man to cover his mouth. [38]

al-Khaṭṭābī said:

> '*Al-saḍl*: letting one's clothes hang down all the way to the ground.' [39]
>
> '*Al-saḍl* is completely forbidden because it has to do with showing off, and in prayer it is even worse.'

The author of *al-Nihāyah* said:

> 'It means wrapping oneself up in one's garment, leaving one's hands inside and bowing and prostrating in it.'
>
> 'It was said that the Jews used to do this.'
>
> 'It was also said that *al-saḍl* meant putting the garment over one's head or shoulders, and letting its edges come down in front and over one's upper arms, so that a person will be preoccupied in taking care of it, which reduces *khushū'*, unlike garments that are tied up properly or buttoned, which do not distract the

---

[38] Reported by Abū Dāwūd, [no. 643]; *Ṣaḥīḥ al-Jāmi'*, [no. 6883]. He said, this is a *ḥasan ḥadīth*. In *'Awn al-Ma'būd* [2/347].

[39] *Marqāt al-Mafātīḥ*, [2/236].

worshipper or affect his *khushū*'.'

These kinds of clothes are still to be found nowadays in some parts of Africa and elsewhere, and in the way some Arabian cloaks are worn, which distract the worshipper and keep him busy adjusting them, retying them if they become loose and so on. This should be avoided.

The reason why it is forbidden to cover one's mouth was explained by the scholars as being because that prevents a person from reciting Qur'ān and doing *sujūd* properly. [40]

Not resembling animals

Allāh has honoured the son of Ādam and created him in the best way, so it is shameful for the son of Ādam to resemble or imitate animals. We have been forbidden to resemble or imitate a number of postures or movements of animals when we pray, because that is contrary to *khushū*' or because it is ugly and does not befit the worshipper who is praying. For example, it was reported that the Messenger of Allāh (ﷺ) forbade three things in prayer: pecking like a crow, spreading oneṛs forearms like a carnivore, or always praying in the same place like a camel keeping to its own territory. [41]

It was said that when a man always prays in the same place in

[40] It was reported in *Marqāt al-Mafātīh*, [2/236].

[41] Reported by Aḥmad, [3/428].

the mosque, making it his own, it is like a camel keeping to its own territory. [42]

According to another report:

> "He forbade me to peck like a cockerel, to sit like a dog or to turn like a fox." [43]

This is what we were able to mention about the means of attaining *khushū'*, so that we may strive for them, and about the things that detract from *khushū'*, so that we can avoid them.

There is another issue that has to do with *khushū'*, to which the scholars attached so much importance that it is worthy of mention here:

---

[42] *Al-Fath al-Rabāni*, [4/91].

[43] Reported by Imām Aḥmad, [2/311]; *Ṣaḥīḥ al-Targhīb*, [no. 556].

GOOD MANNERS AT HOME

Spreading kindness in the home

'Ā'ishah (may Allāh be pleased with her) said: 'The Messenger of Allāh (ﷺ) said:

> "When Allāh - may He be glorified - wills some good towards the people of a household, He introduces kindness among them."' [1]

According to another report:

> "When Allāh loves the people of a household, He introduces kindness among them." [2]

In other words, they start to be kind to one another. This is one of the means of attaining happiness in the home, for kindness is very beneficial between the spouses, and with the children, and brings results that cannot be achieved through harshness, as the Prophet (ﷺ) said:

---

[1] Reported by Imām Aḥmad in *al-Musnad*, [6/71]; *Ṣaḥīḥ al-Jāmi'*, [303].

[2] Reported by Ibn Abī al-Dunyā and others; *Ṣaḥīḥ al-Jāmi'*, [no. 1704].

> "Allāh loves kindness and rewards it in such a way that He does not reward for harshness or for anything else." [3]

Helping one's wife with the housework

Many men think that housework is beneath them, and some of them think that it will undermine their status and position if they help their wives with this work.

The Messenger of Allāh (ﷺ), however, used to

> "sew his own clothes, mend his own shoes and do whatever other work men do in their homes." [4]

This was said by his wife 'Ā'ishah (may Allāh be pleased with her), when she was asked about what the Messenger of Allāh (ﷺ) used to do in his house; her response described what she herself had seen.

According to another report, she said:

> "He was like any other human being: he would clean his clothes, milk his ewe and serve himself." [5]

She (may Allāh be pleased with her) was also asked about what the Messenger of Allāh (ﷺ) used to do in his house, and she

---

[3] Reported by Muslim, *Kitāb al-Birr wa'l-Sillah wa'l-Ādāb,* [no. 2592].

[4] Reported by Imām Aḥmad in *al-Musnad,* [6/121]; *Ṣaḥīḥ al-Jāmi',* 4927].

[5] Reported by Imām Aḥmad in *al-Musnad,* [6/256]; *al-Silsilat al-Ṣaḥīḥah,* [671].

said,

> "He used to serve his family, then when the time for prayer came, he would go out to pray." [6]

If we were to do likewise nowadays, we would achieve three things:

[i]. We would be following the example of the Prophet (ﷺ)
[ii]. We would be helping our wives
[iii]. We would feel more humble, not arrogant.

Some men demand food instantly from their wives, when the pot is on the stove and the baby is screaming to be fed; they do not pick up the child or wait a little while for the food. Let these *aḥādīth* be a reminder and a lesson.

Being affectionate towards and joking with the members of the family

Showing affection towards one's wife and children is one of the things that lead to creating an atmosphere of happiness and friendliness in the home. Thus the Messenger of Allāh (ﷺ) advised Jābir to marry a virgin, saying,

> "Why did you not marry a virgin, so you could play with her and she could play with you, and you could make her laugh and she could make you laugh?" [7]

---

[6] Reported by al-Bukhārī, *al-Fath*, [2/162].

[7] The *ḥadīth* is reported in a number of places in the *Ṣaḥīḥayn*, such as al-Bukhārī, *al-Fath*, [9/121].

The Prophet (ﷺ) also said:

> "Everything in which Allāh's name is not mentioned is idleness and play, except for four things: a man playing with his wife..." [8]

The Prophet (ﷺ) used to treat his wife 'Ā'ishah affectionately when doing *ghusl* with her, as she (may Allāh be pleased with her) said:

> "The Messenger of Allāh and I used to do *ghusl* together from one vessel, and he would pretend to take all the water so that I would say, 'Leave some for me, leave some for me,'" - and both of them were in a state of *janābah* (impurity). [9]

The ways in which the Prophet (ﷺ) showed affection towards young children are too famous to need mentioning. He often used to show his affection towards Ḥasan and Ḥusayn, as mentioned above. This is probably one of the reason why the children used to rejoice when he came back from travelling; they would rush to welcome him, as reported in the *ṣaḥīḥ ḥadīth*:

> "Whenever he came back from a journey, the children of his household would be taken out to meet him."

He (ﷺ) used to hug them close to him, as 'Abd-Allāh ibn Jāfar said:

---

[8] Reported by al-Nisā'i in *'Ushrāt al-Nisā'*, [p. 87]; also in *Ṣaḥīḥ al-Jāmi'*.

[9] Reported by Muslim *bi Sharḥ al-Nawawi,* [4/6].

> "Whenever the Prophet (ﷺ) came back from a journey, we would be taken out to meet him. One day we met him, Ḥasan, Ḥusayn and I. He carried one of us in front of him, and another on his back, until we entered Madīnah." [10]

Compare this with the situation in some miserable homes where there are no truthful jokes [i.e., jokes that do not involve lying], no affection and no mercy. Whoever thinks that kissing his children goes against the dignity of fatherhood should read the following *ḥadīth*: from Abu Hurayrah (may Allāh be pleased with him) who said: "The Messenger of Allāh (ﷺ) kissed al-Ḥasan ibn 'Alī, and al-Aqrā' ibn Hābis al-Tamīmi was sitting with him. Al-Aqrā' said:

> 'I have ten children and I have never kissed any one of them.' The Messenger of Allāh (ﷺ) looked at him and said: 'The one who does not show mercy will not be shown mercy.'"

Resisting bad manners in the home.

Every member of the household is bound to have some bad characteristics, such as lying, backbiting, gossiping and so on. These bad characteristics have to be resisted and opposed.

Some people think that corporal punishment is the only way to deal with such things. The following *ḥadīth* is very educational on this topic: from 'Ā'ishah (may Allāh be pleased with her) who

---

[10] Reported by Muslim, [4/1885-2772]; see the commentary in *Tuḥfāt al-Aḥwadhī*, [8/56].

said:

> "If the Messenger of Allāh (ﷺ) came to know that one of his household had told a lie, he would try to ignore him until he repented." [11]

It is clear from the *ḥadīth* that turning away and forsaking a person by not speaking to them, rather than resorting to punishment, is effective in such circumstances, and may be more effective than physical punishment, so let parents and caregivers think about this.

Hang up the whip

"Hang up the whip where the members of the household can see it." [12]

Hinting at punishment is an effective means of discipline, so the reason for hanging up a whip or stick in the house was explained in another report, where the Prophet (ﷺ) said:

> "Hang up the whip where the members of the household can see it, for this is more effective in disciplining them." [13]

---

[11] See *al-Musnad* by Imaām Aḥmad, [6/152]. The text of the *ḥadīth* is also in *Ṣaḥīḥ al-Jāmi'*, [no. 4675].

[12] Reported by Abū Na'īm in *al-Hilyah*, [7/332]; *al-Silsilat al-Ṣaḥīḥah*, [no. 1446].

[13] Reported by al-Tabarānī, [10/344-345]; *al-Silsilat al-Ṣaḥīḥah*, [no. 1447].

Seeing the means of punishment hanging up will make those who have bad intentions refrain from indulging in bad behaviour, lest they get a taste of the punishment. It will motivate them to behave themselves and be good-mannered.

Ibn al-Anbārī said:

> 'There is nothing to suggest that it should be used for hitting, because [the Prophet (ﷺ)] did not command anyone to do that. What he meant was: keep on disciplining them.' [14]

Hitting is not the way to discipline; it is not to be resorted to, except when all other means are exhausted, or when it is needed to force someone to do obligatory acts of obedience, as Allāh says:

وَٱلَّٰتِي تَخَافُونَ
نُشُوزَهُنَّ فَعِظُوهُنَّ وَٱهۡجُرُوهُنَّ فِي ٱلۡمَضَاجِعِ
وَٱضۡرِبُوهُنَّۖ فَإِنۡ أَطَعۡنَكُمۡ فَلَا تَبۡغُواْ عَلَيۡهِنَّ سَبِيلًاۗ

> **...As to those women on whose part you fear ill-conduct, admonish them (first), (next), refuse to share their beds, (and last) beat them (lightly, if it is useful)...**
>
> [*al-Nisā'* (4) : 34]

There is also the *ḥadīth*:

> "Order your children to pray when they are seven

[14] See *Fayd al-Qadīr* by al-Mannāwī, [4/325].

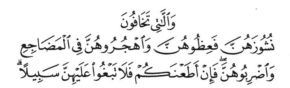

> years old, and hit them if they do not do so when they are ten." [15]

As for hitting unnecessarily, this is aggression. The Messenger of Allāh (ﷺ) advised a woman not to marry a man because he always had his stick on his shoulder, i.e., he used to beat his wives. On the other hand, there are those who think that they should never use this method of discipline at all, following some *kāfir* educational theories; this is also a mistaken opinion that goes against the *sharī'ah.*

[15] *Sunan Abī Dāwūd,* [1/334]; see also *Irwā' al-Ghalīl,* [1/266].

EVILS IN THE HOME

Putting things right in the home is a great trust and huge responsibility which every Muslim man and woman should undertake as Allāh commands; they should run the affairs of their homes in accordance with the rules set out by Allāh. One of the ways of achieving this is by ridding the home of evil things. The following aims to highlight some evil things that actually happen in some homes and that have become tools of destruction for the nests in which the future generations of the Muslim ummah are being raised.

This in brief highlights some of these evil things, explaining about some *harām* things in order to warn about them. It is a gift to every seeker of truth who is looking for methods of change, so that he or she can implement the command of the Messenger of Allāh (ﷺ):

> "Whoever of you sees an evil action, let him change it with his hand [by taking action], and if he cannot, then with his tongue [by speaking out], and if he cannot, then with his heart [by feeling that it is wrong] - and that is the weakest of faith." [1]

---

1 Reported by Muslim in his *Ṣaḥīḥ*, [1/69].

Beware of allowing non-*mahram* relatives to enter upon the wife

Beware of allowing non-*mahram* relatives to enter upon the wife in the home when the husband is absent. Some homes are not free of the presence of relatives of the husband who are not *mahram* for the wife, who may be living in his home with him because of some social circumstances, such as his brothers who may be students or single. These relatives enter the home without anyone raising an eyebrow, because they are known in the neighbourhood as being relatives of the head of the household, his brothers or nephews or uncles. This relaxed attitude could generate a lot of evil which will earn the wrath of Allāh if it is not controlled and brought within the limits set by Allāh. The basic principle in this matter is the *ḥadīth* of the Prophet (ﷺ),

> "Beware of entering upon women." A man from among the Anṣār said, "O Messenger of Allāh, what do you think about the brother-in-law?" He said, "The brother-in-law is death!" [2]

Al-Nawāwī said:

> 'What is referred to in this hadeeth is the husband's relatives apart from his father and his sons, because those are *mahrams* for his wife and can be alone with her, so they are not described as death. What is referred to here is his brother, nephew, uncle and cousin, and others who she would be permitted to marry if she were not already married. Usually people take the matter lightly with regard to these relatives, so a brother

[2] Reported by al-Bukhārī, *Fath al-Bārī*, [9/330].

> may be alone with his brother's wife. Thus he is likened to death, when he should be prevented from being alone with her more than a stranger should.' [3]

The phrase *'the brother-in-law is death'* has a number of meanings, such as:

That being alone with the brother-in-law may lead to spiritual destruction if she commits sin;

Or it may lead to death if she commits the immoral act (*zinā* or adultery) and the punishment of stoning is carried out on her;

Or it may lead to the woman being destroyed if her husband leaves her because his jealousy leads him to divorce her; Or it may mean, beware of being alone with a non-*mahram* woman just as you would beware of death; Or it may mean that being alone with a non-*mahram* woman is as bad as death.

It was said that it means, let the brother-in-law die rather than be alone with a non-*mahram* woman,

All of this stems from the concern of Islām to preserve families and households, and to prevent the tools of destruction reaching them in the first place. Having learned what the Prophet (ﷺ) said, what do you think now of those husbands who tell their wives,

"If my brother comes and I am not here, let him into the sitting room",
or a wife who tells a guest, "Go into the sitting room"

---

[3] *Fath al-Bārī*, [9/331].

when there is no one else present in the house?

To those who raise the issue of trust as an excuse, saying 'I trust my wife, and I trust my brother, or my cousin', we say: your trust is all well and good, and you should not be suspicious when you have no cause to do so, but you should know that the *ḥadīth* of the Prophet (ﷺ),

> "No man is alone with a non-*mahram* woman, but the *Shayṭān* is the third one present with them." [4]

Includes the most pious of people as well as the most corrupt. Islaam does not exempt anyone from such rulings.

Whilst writing these few lines, we heard about a problematic situation in which, to cut a long story short, a man married a woman and brought her to live in his family home, where she lived happily with him. Then his younger brother began to enter upon her when her husband was absent, and talk to her in a romantic manner, which resulted in two things: firstly, she began to dislike her husband intensely, and secondly, she fell in love with his brother. But she was not able to divorce her husband, nor was she able to do what she wanted with the other man. This is the grievous penalty. This story illustrates one level of corruption, beyond which there are many more which culminate in the immoral action (*zinā*/adultery) and the birth of illegitimate children.

[4] Reported by al-Tirmidhī, [1171].

Segregating men and women in family visits

Man is naturally gregarious and sociable; he needs friends and friendships entail visiting one another.

When there are visits between families, we should block the path of evil by not mixing. One of the indications that mixing is haraam is the *āyah*:

وَإِذَا سَأَلْتُمُوهُنَّ مَتَٰعًا فَسْـَٔلُوهُنَّ مِن
وَرَآءِ حِجَابٍ ۚ ذَٰلِكُمْ أَطْهَرُ لِقُلُوبِكُمْ وَقُلُوبِهِنَّ

...And when you ask his wives) for anything you want, ask them from behind a screen, that is purer for your hearts and for their hearts...

[*al-Aḥzāb* (33) : 53]

If we were to look for the evil results of mixing during family visits, we would find many objectionable things, such as:

[i]. In most cases the *hijāb* of women in these mixed gatherings is non-existent or is not proper, so a woman may display her beauty before someone in front of whom it is not permissible for her to uncover herself. Allāh says:

وَقُل لِّلْمُؤْمِنَٰتِ
يَغْضُضْنَ مِنْ أَبْصَٰرِهِنَّ وَيَحْفَظْنَ فُرُوجَهُنَّ

And tell the believing women... not to reveal their adornment...

[*al-Nūr* (24) : 31]

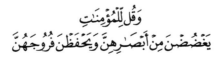

It may happen that a woman adorns herself for strangers in a mixed gathering in a way that she never does for her husband.

[ii]. When men see women in one gathering, this is a cause of corruption in the religion and morals, and provokes desires in a forbidden manner.

[iii]. The spouses may argue and ignore one another in an alarming fashion, when one looks at or winks at another man's wife, or laughs and jokes with her, and she with him. After a couple returns home, the settling of scores begins:

> Man: Why did you laugh at what so and so said, when he did not say anything funny?
> Woman: And why did you wink at so and so?
> Man: When he spoke, you understood him quickly, but you do not understand what I say at all!

Thus they trade accusations and the matter ends in enmity and even divorce.

[iv]. Some men and woman may regret their luck in marriage, when a man compares his wife to his friend's wife, or a woman compares her husband to her friend's husband. A man may say to himself: 'So and so talks and answers questions... she is well-educated and my wife is ignorant, she has no education...' and a woman may say to herself, 'So and so is so lucky! Her husband is smart and eloquent, and my husband is so boring and speaks without thinking.' This spoils the marital relationship or leads to bad treatment.

[v]. Some people may show off to one another by pretending to have things that they don't really have. So a man may issue

instructions to his wife in front of other men and pretend that he has a strong personality, but when he is alone with her at home he is like a tame pussycat. A woman may borrow gold and wear it so that the other people may see that she has such and such. But the Prophet (ﷺ) said:

> "The one who shows off with something that does not belong to him is like one who wears a garment of falsehood." [5]

[vi]. These late-night mixed gatherings result in wasted time, sins of the tongue, and leaving small children home alone (so that they do not disturb the evening with their cries!)

[vii]. These late-night mixed gatherings may even develop to the extent of involving many kinds of major sins, such as drinking wine and gambling, especially among the so-called 'upper classes'. One of the major sins that occur during these gatherings is following the *kuffār* and imitating them in fashions and various customs.

The Messenger of Allāh (ﷺ) said,

> "Whoever imitates a people is one of them." [6]

---

[5] Reported by al-Bukhārī, *al-Fath*, [9/317].

[6] Reported by Imām Aḥmad in *al-Musnad*, [2/50]; *Ṣaḥīḥ al-Jāmi'*, [2828], [6025].

Beware of the dangers of having (male) drivers and (female) servants in the home.

Striving to ward off evil is a religious duty, and closing the doors of evil and *fitnah* (temptation) is one of the priorities of *sharī'ah*. A lot of *fitnah* and sin has come to us through servants and drivers, but many people do not pay attention to this, and if they do notice it, they do not take it seriously. A person may be stung repeatedly from the same place, but he does not feel the pain, or he may hear of a disaster that happened near his own home, but he does not learn from it. This stems from weak faith and the failure to feel that Allaah is near, failings that affect the hearts of many people in the modern age. We will briefly explain the bad effects of having servants and drivers in the home, so that it will be a reminder to the one who has the eyes to see or who wants to follow the right path in his own home.

Having female servants in the home presents men, especially young ones, with *fitnah* and temptation, through their adornment and being alone with them. We hear so many stories, one after another, of some youth being led astray, and the reason for this is that the servant entered upon a young man, or a young man took advantage of the fact that no one else was home and entered upon the servant. Some young men have told their families frankly about what happened, and the families did not respond; in other cases the family may have discovered something, but their response was bereft of any sense of honour or jealousy.

يُوسُفُ أَعْرِضْ عَنْ
هَٰذَا وَٱسْتَغْفِرِى لِذَنۢبِكِ إِنَّكِ كُنتِ مِنَ ٱلْخَاطِـِٔينَ

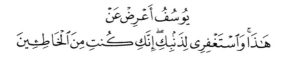

O Yūsuf! Turn away from this! (O woman!) Ask forgiveness for your sin. Verily, you were of the sinful.

[*Yūsuf* (12) : 29]

So the fire remains close to the fuel, and the situation is left as it is, with no changes being made. It has also happened that servants have taught misbehaviour to the daughters of the household.

• The lady of the house neglects her duties and forgets her responsibilities, and becomes accustomed to being lazy, then when the servants travels things are very hard indeed for her.

• The children receive a bad upbringing, represented by the following examples:

The children learn the beliefs of *kufr* from *kāfir* servants, Christians and Buddhists. There have been children who make the sign of the cross on their heads and two sides of their chests, as they have seen a Christian woman doing when she prays, and she tells them, 'This is something sweet from Christ.' Or a child may see a servant praying to a statue of Buddha, or another celebrating her people's festivals and conveying to our children her feelings of joy, so they get used to taking part in festivals of *kufr*.

The children are deprived of their mother's love and care, which is an essential part of their upbringing and psychological stability. A servant cannot make up this lack for a child who is not hers.

The child's Arabic will be corrupted because it is mixed with foreign words, so he grows up lacking something, which will have an adverse effect on his education in school.

Some heads of households feel the financial strain of paying salaries for drivers and servants. Then there are the family disputes that arise over who should pay these salaries, especially in cases where the wife is employed. If the wife would stay at home instead of working outside the home, she would spare herself a lot of trouble. The fact of the matter is that in many cases we create trouble for ourselves, then we demand a solution, and often the solution we come up with is far from decisive.

Getting used to having servants has created dependency and negative character traits.

Some women may include having a servant as a condition in their marriage contract; others may plan on bringing their family's servant with them when they get married. Thus our daughters have lost the ability to deal independently with anything in the home, no matter how small it is.

• When women brought servants into their homes, they started to have a lot of free time and did not know what to do with it. So some women began to sleep a lot, and some are never home because they are always going to gatherings where they gossip and backbite and waste their time. The result will be regret on the Day of Resurrection.

• Harm comes to the members of the family in different ways, for example:

[i]-Witchcraft and magic, which can cause the separation of hus-

band and wife, or cause physical harm.

[ii]-Harm to the possessions of family members because of theft.

[iii]-Damage to the family's reputation. How many decent homes have been turned into dens of immorality and corruption in the absence of their owners. You must surely have heard of female servants who receive men when the homeowners are absent.

• The freedom of men (those who fear Allāh) within their own homes is restricted, as is also the case for those who try to call their families to put things in order.

• Women end up being alone with drivers who are strangers (non-*mahrams*) to them, in the house or car, and women do not refrain from going out wearing adornments and perfume in front of the drivers. They act as if he is one of their *mahrams* or even closer, and because they go out with them so often and talk to them so much, the psychological barrier is broken down and so forbidden things are done. The frequency of such incidents in our society demonstrates to those who have the eyes to see just how serious the matter is.

• Bringing servants and drivers from all sorts of *kāfir* nations clearly goes against the Prophet's specific orders that *kāfirs* should not be allowed into the Arabian Peninsula. There is absolutely no need to do this, as it is possible to bring Muslims in if there is a need for workers. Added to this is the fact that employing *kāfirs* strengthens the economies of *kāfir* nations, as the employees transfer their salaries to their homelands, even though Muslims should have priority in this matter. By mixing so much with these *kāfirs*, Muslims can no longer see the difference, which gradually destroys the concept of *al-walā wa'l-barā'* (loyalty and allegiance vs. enmity and disavowal) in their minds.

Added to this is the ugly role played by some agency owners who have no fear of Allāh, who will tell you that there are no Muslim employees. Or they may engage in deceit and trickery, so that after a driver or servant who is described as a Muslim in official papers has arrived, the head of the household discovers that this is a lie, or the new employee may be playing a role that started in his country of origin, where the agency taught him a few Islamic words so that he can pose as a Muslim in front of the family that employs him.

• Family breakup resulting from the householder's affair with a female servant. Look at what really happens and think how many divorces have happened because of servants, and how many servants have become pregnant with illegitimate children.

Then ask the people working in hospital maternity departments, or find out about police reports detailing the problems caused by illegitimate children born as a result of the temptation posed by female servants. Then try to understand the extent of the spread of venereal diseases which have been brought into our society because of that. Now you will understand the vicious circle we are in because of bringing female servants into our homes.

Think about the misconceptions that these servants and drivers have about the Islāmic religion when they see the behaviour of those who claim to be Muslim.

Ask yourself, what kind of obstacles are we placing in front of them? How are we preventing them from discovering the way of

Allāh by what we do to them? How could they possibly enter a religion when this is the state of those who claim to belong to it?

Because of these matters and others, some scholars think that it is not permissible to bring female servants into the home in the manner in which this is done nowadays, and that it is obligatory to put a stop to *fitnah* and close the door to evil. [7]

In order to comply with the command of Allāh:

وَإِذَا قُلْتُمْ فَاعْدِلُوا۟

..and when you give your word, say the truth...
[*al-An'ām* (6) :152]

we should point out the following:

Firstly: we do not deny the fact that some servants and drivers are sincere Muslims, possibly more sincere than the members of the household. We have heard of a servant who keeps a *Mus-ḥaf* (copy of the Qur'ān) on the shelf in the kitchen so that she can read it whenever she finishes her work, and a driver who prays Fajr in the mosque before his employer does.

Secondly: we are not ignoring the real needs that people sometimes have for essential reasons, such as needing the help of servants in a large house, or when a family has a lot of children, or when someone is chronically ill or has disabilities, or when there is hard work that the wife cannot do on her own. But what we Muslims should ask is: who is applying Islāmic conditions and

---

[7] See the *fatwā* of Shaykh Muḥammad ibn Sāliḥ al-'Uthaymīn on this issue.

taking care of religious precautions when bringing servants and drivers into the home? How many of those who bring drivers into the home (let's get real!) can guarantee that the driver will not be alone with one of his womenfolk, or that the man will not be alone with a female servant? He should also tell the female servant to observe *hijāb*, and he should not deliberately look at her adornment. If he comes home and no one is there but the servant, he should not enter. He should not accept any servants except those who are sincerely Muslim... and so on.

For this reason, everyone who has one of these servants or drivers in his home should make sure that this person is there for a legitimate need and that the Islamic conditions are being properly fulfilled. The story of Yūsuf (upon whom be peace) contains a lesson for us with regard to this matter. It clearly indicates the *fitnah* that exists when there are servants and drivers in the house, and that evil may be initiated by members of the household even though the servants are people who fear Allāh. Allāh says:

وَرَٰوَدَتْهُ ٱلَّتِي هُوَ فِي بَيْتِهَا عَن نَّفْسِهِۦ وَغَلَّقَتِ ٱلْأَبْوَٰبَ
وَقَالَتْ هَيْتَ لَكَ ۚ قَالَ مَعَاذَ ٱللَّهِ ۖ

And she, in whose house he was, sought to seduce him (to do an evil act), she closed the doors and said: 'Come on, O you.' He said, 'I seek refuge in Allāh (or Allāh forbid)!'...

[*Yūsuf* (12) : 23]

We suggest to those who complain that things are too difficult in their homes without servants that they could do the following:

• Buy ready-made food from the market; use paper plates; use laundry services; have the house cleaned by workers who are supervised by the man; ask relatives to help care for the children when necessary, such as when the wife is recovering from childbirth.

• If that is not enough, they could seek the help of a temporary servant, under proper Islāmic conditions, and when there is no longer any need she may be dismissed. There are, however, risks attached to this solution.

• It is better if the servant is paid hourly, so that she can do her job then leave the house. Whatever the case, things should be done only as they are needed.

• We have discussed this matter at length because the problem is so widespread in our society. It may be different in other countries. Before closing this discussion we should mention some matters that have to do with *taqwā* or fear of Allāh:

1- Everyone who has sources of *fitnah* in his home, whether from servants or from anything else, should fear Allāh and remove them from his home.

2- Everyone who thinks that he is going to impose Islāmic conditions when bringing a servant to his home should fear Allāh and realize that many of these conditions will become less stringent as time goes by.

3- Everyone who has a *kāfir* servant in the Arabian Peninsula should present Islām to him or her in the best possible way. If he or she becomes Muslim, all well and good, otherwise the servant should be sent back to wherever he or she came from.

Finally, we will end this discussion on servants and drivers with a story that contains an important lesson about the dangers of having servants in the home, and about referring to the Qur'ān and Sunnah, and rejecting every ruling that contradicts the *sharī'ah*, and consulting people of knowledge, and purifying the Islāmic society through application of the punishments prescribed by Allāh.

Abū Hurayrah and Zayd ibn Khālid (may Allāh be pleased with them) said:

> "We were with the Prophet (ﷺ) when a man stood up and said, 'I urge you by Allāh to judge between us according to the Book of Allāh.' His opposite number, who was more knowledgeable, stood up and said, 'Judge between us according to the Book of Allāh and give me permission to speak.' The Prophet (ﷺ) said, 'Speak.' He said, 'This son of mine was employed as a servant by this man, and committed *zinā* (adultery) with his wife. I gave him one hundred sheep and a servant in compensation [for the damage to his honour], then I consulted some of those who have knowledge, and they told me that my son should be flogged one hundred times and exiled for a year [because he was unmarried], and that the woman should be stoned [because she was married and she consented to the act].' The Prophet (ﷺ) said: 'By the One in Whose hand is my soul, I will judge between you according to the Book of Allāh. Take back the hundred sheep and the servant. Your son is to be flogged one hundred times and exiled for one year. O Unays, go to this man's wife tomorrow and if she

> confesses, then stone her.' [Unays] went to her the next day and she confessed, so he stoned her." [8]

One of the things that upsets every Muslim who cares about the rulings of Islām is what happens in some homes, where cleaners and maintenance workers enter upon women when they are wearing nightdresses and house-dresses. Does these women think that these people are not men in front of whom Allāh has commanded them to observe *hijāb*?

Another evil thing that happens in some homes is where non-*mahram* men teach adolescent girls, or some women teach adolescent boys without wearing *hijāb*.

---

[8] Reported by al-Bukhārī, *al-Fath*, [12/136].

Expelling effeminate men from our homes

al-Bukhārī (may Allāh have mercy on him) reported, in his chapter on expelling men who imitate women from our homes, the *ḥadīth* of Ibn ʻAbbās, who said:

> "The Prophet (ﷺ) cursed men who imitate women and women who imitate men, and said, 'Expel t hem from your homes.' The Prophet (ﷺ) expelled so and so [a man]. And ʻUmar expelled so and so [a woman]." [9]

Then al-Bukhārī quoted the *ḥadīth* of Umm Salamah, which he reported under the title 'What is forbidden of men who imitate women entering upon women':

From Umm Salamah, who said that the Prophet (ﷺ) was in her house, where there was also an effeminate man who told her brother ʻAbd-Allāh ibn Abī Umayyah:

> 'If Allāh wills that you conquer al-Ṭā'if tomorrow, I will show you the daughter of Ghaylān; she has four folds of fat in front and eight behind.' The Prophet (ﷺ) said, "This person should not enter upon you."'"[10]

The definition of *'effeminate man'* (*mukhannath*): this is a man who may resemble women physically, or by imitating their movements and speech, and so on. If it is physical, i.e., this is the way

[9] Reported by al-Bukhārī in *Kitāb al-Libās*, [chapter 62], *al-Fath*, [10/333].

[10] Reported by al-Bukhārī, [chapter 113], *al-Fath*, [9/333].

that he is made, then there is no blame on him, but he must try as much as he can to change this resemblance. If he is imitating women deliberately, then he is described as *mukhannath* (effeminate) whether he commits the evil deed (is a homosexual) or not.

The effeminate man referred to here - who was like a servant - used to enter the houses of the Messenger of Allāh (ﷺ) because he was considered to be;

> "an old male servant who lacked vigour." [11]

When the Messenger (ﷺ) realized that this person could describe women very precisely and that he was describing a woman as having four folds of fat in front and eight behind (four on each side), he ordered that he should be thrown out and not allowed to enter his wives apartments, because of the mischief that he could cause, such as possibly describing the women he saw to strangers, or having a bad influence on the members of the household, such as leading women to imitate men, or men to imitate women by walking in a coquettish manner or speaking softly, or worse mischief than that.

So how about the situation nowadays, when we see many of these servants imitating the opposite sex, especially the *kāfirs* who are living in Muslim homes and who we know for sure are having a bad influence on Muslim boys and girls. There is even a group known as *'the third sex'*, who wear make up and dress in women's clothes. What a disaster for the nation which is supposed to be the *ummah* of *jihād*!

---

[11] See. *Sūrah al-Nūr* (24) : 31.

If you want to know more about how the Prophet (ﷺ) opposed this *'the third sex'* and how his Companions fought with their sense of honour against such things, think about this *ḥadīth*:

Abū Hurayrah (may Allāh be pleased with him) reported that an effeminate man who had dyed his hands with *henna* (as women do) was brought to the Prophet (ﷺ), and it was said,

> "O Messenger of Allāh! This man is imitating women." So he banished him to *al-Baqī'* (as a punishment, sending him to an isolated place, and to protect others). It was said, "Why do you not kill him?" He said, "I have been forbidden to kill those who pray." [12]

---

[12] Reported by Abū Dāwūd, [4928,] and others. See *Ṣaḥīḥ al-Jāmi'*, [2502].

Beware of the dangers of the small screen

Hardly any home nowadays is free of some device that includes a screen [TV and computers], and very few of these machines are used for wholesome or beneficial purposes. Mostly they are used for harmful and destructive things, especially VCRs used for watching movies. With the arrival of satellite dishes which bring shows directly into Muslim homes and the widespread sale and exchange of movies, the matter of controlling these devices has become nearly impossible.

There follows a list of some of the harmful and corrupting effects that result from watching TV etc. After thinking about them, let everyone who wants to earn the pleasure of Allaah and avoid His wrath do what he can to change the situation:

i. Impact on our faith (*ʿaqīdah*):

- Showing the symbols of the *kuffār* and their false religious signs, such as the cross, Buddha, their temples, gods and goddesses of love, good, evil, light, distress and rain. There are also missionary movies that call on people to venerate the religion of Christianity and become Christians.

- Giving the impression that some created beings could compete with Allāh in creating and giving life and death, such as some scenes which show people bringing the dead back to life by using a cross or magic wand.

- Spreading lies, myths, legends, witchcraft, fortune-telling and soothsaying, all of which contradict *Tawḥīd.*

• Giving the impression that we should show respect to the representatives of false religions, such as the pope, bishops and nuns who treat the sick and do good!

• In many dramas, characters swear by things other than Allāh, or play with the names of Allāh, such as when one character called another 'Abd al-Qīsāh. [13]

• Causing doubts about Allāh's power, or His ability to create; or portraying life as a conflict between Allāh and man.

• Those who watch such things lose the concept of disavowing oneself and distancing oneself from the enemies of Allāh, because these shows and movies portray things that make them admire the characters of the *kuffār* and their societies, and break down the psychological barriers between Muslims and *kuffār.* Once the idea of hatred for the sake of Allāh is removed, they begin to imitate these *kuffār* and take new ideas from them.

ii. Social impact

• Admiration of *kuffār* characters when they are shown as heroes in these films.

[13] This implies disrespect towards Allāh by toying with names that mean 'slave of [Allāh]' - which are among the best names that a person can have. For example, 'Abd al-Raḥmān means 'slave of the Most Merciful', 'Abd al-Ḥakīm means 'slave of the Most Wise' and so on, but 'Abd al-Qīsāh means nothing and makes a mockery of such names.

• Propagation of crime, through showing scenes of violence, murders, kidnap and rape.

• Forming gangs as is shown in films, to commit acts of aggression and crimes. Youth detention centres and jails bear witness to the impact of the movies in this regard.

• Learning the arts of cheating, fraud and forgery, taking bribes, and other kinds of major sins.

• Calling for women to imitate men and vice versa, which clearly goes against the *ḥadīth* of the Prophet (ﷺ) in which he cursed those who do such things. So we may see a man imitating the way a woman walks and talks, wearing a wig and jewellery, using dyes and make-up. Or we may see a woman wearing a false beard or moustache, and making her voice deep. This is one of the causes of promiscuity in society and the emergence of the *'third sex'*.

• Instead of taking the Prophet (ﷺ), *Sahābah*, scholars and *mujāḥidīn* as examples, people follow actors, singers, dancers and sports players.

• Men no longer feel any sense of responsibility towards their families, so important needs are ignored and sick children are neglected, because the head of the family is glued to the TV and may even hit a child harshly if he dares to interrupt his viewing of a movie.

• Rebellion of children against their parents, as is propagated on TV and in the movies. If a child insists on taking money from his father, and his father reminds him of the rights he has, the child in a TV drama may say, 'Just because you are my father does it mean that you can rip me off?!' But the Prophet (ﷺ) said,

"You and your wealth belong to your father." [14]

• Breakdown of family ties, because people are too busy watching movies to visit one another. When they do visit, they do not have any kind of useful conversation or discuss solutions to family problems because they are gathered around the screen, silently watching.

• People are distracted from taking care of their guests properly.

• Spread of laziness and idleness and reduction in productivity, because the TV takes up the Muslim's time.

• Marital discord and mutual hatred; outbreaks of reprehensible jealousy, as when a man praises the beauty of a woman on TV in front of his wife, and she responds by mentioning a handsome actor or newscaster.

• Absence of the proper kind of jealousy (*ghīrah*), because people get used to watching scenes of mixing, wives being uncovered in front of non-*mahram* men and unveiling of daughters and sisters, and they are influenced by calls for womenṟs liberation.

[14] Reported by Abū Dāwūd, [3530].

iii. Moral impact

- Provoking desires by showing pictures of women to men, and images of handsome men to women.

- Calling society to show that which should be hidden by promoting revealing clothes and getting people used to seeing them.

- Calling for relationships between the sexes and teaching people how to get to know the opposite sex, what sort of words should be exchanged in the beginning, means of developing the forbidden relationship, telling stories of love and passion and holding hands... etc.

- Falling into immorality and *zinā* because of films which portray such things. Some people even reenact what they see in the movies with some of their *maḥram* relatives, may Allāh protect us, or do bad things whilst watching these films.

- Teaching women different kinds of dances which reveal their *ʿawrāt* and are tempting to men. This is a kind of promiscuity and deviation.

- Developing a joking personality and no longer taking anything seriously, in addition to the fact that too much laughter corrupts the heart, because of comedy films.

- Spread of foul language which is used in many movies and TV shows.

- Making people miss *Fajr* prayers because they stay up late at night to watch what is being shown on the screen.

• Causing people to pray late, not to mention causing men to miss the prayers in the *masjid*, because their hearts are too attached to some soap opera, movie or sports match.

• Causing people to hate some acts of worship, as sometimes happens when an exciting match is interrupted so that people can go and pray.

• Reducing the reward of some of those who fast, or causing their reward to be lost altogether, because of the sin of watching these haraam things.

• Criticism of some of the rulings brought by *sharī'ah*, such as hijaab and polygyny.

iv. Historical impact

• Distorting Islāmic history and covering up the facts; failing to mention the achievements of Muslims in movies that speak about human history.

• Distorting proven historical facts, by showing oppressors as if they are oppressed, such as claiming that the Jews have a just cause.

• Belittling the heroes of Islām in the eyes of viewers, as in some dramas or movies where actors play the roles of *Sahābah*, leaders of Islamic conquests or scholars and portray these personalities in an improper manner, mixing the story with love scenes, where the actors are immoral and corrupt in the first place.

• Subjecting the Muslims to psychological defeat and spreading fear among them by showing different kinds of advanced weaponry in the hands of the *kāfirs* and making the Muslims feel that it is not possible to defeat them.

v. Psychological impact:

• Acquiring aggressive and violent attitudes from watching wrestling and violent action films with scenes of bloodshed, bullets and sharp weapons.

• Instilling fear in the hearts of those who watch horror movies, so that a person may wake up screaming because of the dreams he has seen as a result of some scene that has stuck in his memory.

• Distortion of children's and adults' sense of reality by watching unreal scenes, because Allāh has dictated that there should be cause and effect. An example of this is some of the unreal scenes shown in cartoons, which have an effect on children's behaviour in real life.

vi. Impact on health

• Harm caused to eyesight, which is a blessing about which each person will be questioned.

• Increasing the rate of heartbeat, raising blood pressure and heightening nervous tension and so on, when watching horror movies and scenes of bloodshed.

• Late nights cause harm to the body, and each person will be asked on the Day of Resurrection how he used his body.

• Physical harm caused to children when they imitate Superman and the Man of Iron and others; harm caused to adults when they imitate boxers and wrestlers.

vii. Financial impact:

• Spending money on buying TVs and films, paying for repairs and improvements and receiving equipment [dishes, descrambling devices, etc.]. A person will be asked about this money on the Day of Resurrection: what did he spend it on?

• Many people rush to buy extras that they do not need, or they compete in buying clothes because of the advertisements etc. that they see on the screen.

Beware of the evils of the telephone

The telephone is a useful invention, and is one of the essentials of modern life; it saves time, spans distances and keeps you in touch with everybody. It can be used for good purposes, such as waking people up for *Fajr* prayers, asking about *shar'i* matters and seeking *fatwas*, making appointments with good people, upholding the ties of kinship and advising the Muslims.

But at the same time the telephone may also be a means of doing many evil things. How often has the phone been the cause of complete wrecking of a home, the source of misery and suffering for family members and the impetus for men and women to do evil and cause mischief! The danger lies in the ease of use, for it is a direct route from the outside into the heart of the home.

Among the evil uses to which the telephone may be put are:

[i]- Disturbing nuisance calls.

[ii]- Women getting to know strange (non-*mahram*) men, and the development of such relationships. A young man whom Allāh had guided to the path of repentance told me that when a young man gets to know a young woman by phone, she usually ends up going out with him, and whatever immorality follows on from that, only Allāh knows.

[iii]- Wives may be turned against husbands and vice versa, or parents may be turned against their sons and daughters, and vice versa, because of telephone calls from trouble makers, resulting from *ḥasad* (destructive envy) and the love of evil and causing

division among people.

[iv]- Wasting time in idle conversations that harden the heart and turn people away from remembering Allāh. This is a problem especially among women, as they find it a way to get things off their chests.

Solutions to the phone problem include the following:

[i]- Watching out for misuse of the phone inside and outside the home.

[ii]- Using wisdom when answering the phone.

[iii]- When we hear news from someone we do not know, we should deal with it according to the Book of Allāh and obey His command:

فَتَبَيَّنُوٓاْ

...verify it...

[*al-Ḥujurāt* (49) : 6]

[iv]- A sound Islāmic education will guarantee proper use of the telephone when the person who is in charge is absent. [i.e., if children and youth are taught properly, they will not misuse the telephone when their parents and elders are not around].

5- The last resort is to disconnect the phone if the evils it causes are greater than the benefits it brings.

Removing from our homes all symbols of false religion

We have to remove from our homes all symbols of false *kāfir* religions and images of their gods and idols.

'Ā'ishah (may Allāh be pleased with her) reported that the Prophet (ﷺ) would never leave anything in his house that had crosses on it except he would destroy it.[15]

Nowadays we are suffering from having manufactured goods which we bring from the *kāfir* countries, which include images and engravings, and drawings of their gods and idols. This includes various kinds of crosses, pictures of Jesus and Mary, pictures of churches, statues of Buddha, Greek gods like the goddesses of love and good and evil, and so on.

It is not right for the home of the monotheistic Muslim to have in it the symbols of *shirk* that contradict *Tawḥīd* and destroy its foundations. Thus the Prophet (ﷺ) used to destroy crosses if he saw them in his house, by blotting them out if they drawn or engraved, or by scratching them out or covering them in some other way, or getting rid of them altogether.

This is not religious extremism, because the one who forbade people to go to extremes - the Prophet (ﷺ) - did this himself. Hence when family members want to buy vessels or mattresses, etc., they should beware of these symbols of false religions that contradict *Tawḥīd*. At the same time we must point out the importance of being moderate in this matter; if the form is not

---

[15] Reported by al-Bukhārī, *Fath al-Bārī*, [10/385], *Bāb Naqd al-Suwar.*

obviously a cross, for example, it does not have to be changed.

Removing pictures of animate beings

Many people decorate their homes by deliberately hanging pictures on their walls and putting statues on shelves in some corners of the house. Many of these images, whether they are three-dimensional or otherwise, include animate beings such as people, birds, animals and so on.

The statements of scholars who are well-versed in the matter clearly state that static images of animate beings are *harām*, whether they are engraved or drawn or produced by machines - unlike images reflected by mirrors or in water. The *ḥadīth* of the Prophet (ﷺ) which curses image makers and threatens them with being asked to do something that is beyond them, namely breathing life into their images, on the Day of Resurrection, includes everyone who works in the field of photography, except in cases where images are necessary, such as ID photos and photos used in the hunt for criminals, and so on.

Hanging up pictures of animate beings also comprises another sin which could lead to the person venerating the picture and falling into the sin of *shirk*, as happened to the people of (Prophet) Nūḥ. The least harm that hanging up pictures may do is to renew people's grief or lead them to boast and feel too proud of their fathers and grandfathers. No one should say 'We are not prostrating to the picture!'

Whoever wants to deprive himself of the great blessing of having the angels enter his home, let him put pictures up. The Messenger of Allāh (ﷺ) said,

> "The house in which there are images, the angels will not enter it." [16]

There are many *aḥādīth* which forbid making images, such as:

> "The people who will be most severely punished by Allāh on the Day of Resurrection will be the makers of images." [17]

'Abd-Allāh ibn 'Umar reported that the Messenger of Allāh (ﷺ) said:

> "Those who make these images will be punished on the Day of Resurrection. It will said to them, 'Bring to life that which you have created!'" [18]

Abu Hurayrah entered a house in Madīnah and saw something hanging on the wall which was engraved with forbidden images. He said,

> 'I heard the Messenger of Allāh (ﷺ) say, "[Allāh says:] Who is more wrong than the one who tries to create something like My creation? Let them create a grain or an ant!"' [19]

Abu Juhayfah reported that the Prophet (ﷺ) cursed the maker

---

[16] Reported by al-Bukhāri, [4/325].

[17] Reported by al-Bukhārī, [1/382].

[18] Reported by al-Bukhārī, [1/382].

[19] Reported by al-Bukhārī, [1/385].

of images. [20]

If you want more information on this issue, you may consult the books of the scholars.

In the commentary on the *ḥadīth* which says that the angels will not enter a house where there are images, it says:

> "What is meant by 'house' is the place where a person stays, whether it is a building, a tent or anything else." [21]

The images which prevent the angels entering a house are images of animate beings that do not have the heads removed or are not subjected to disrespectful usage (usage such as being stepped on, etc., that makes it clear this image is not being venerated in any way). [22]

Making images of animate beings is a new thing innovated by those who worship images, which includes what the people of (Prophet) Nūḥ did. 'Ā'ishah narrated a *ḥadīth* in which she told the story of the church in Abyssinia (Ethiopia), and the images inside it; she said that the Prophet (ﷺ) said:

> "When a righteous man among them died, they used to build a place of worship over his grave and put these images inside it; those are the most evil of peo-

---

[20] Reported by al-Bukhārī, [1/393].

[21] *Fath al-Bārī*, [1/393].

[22] *al-Fath*, [1/382].

ple in the sight of Allāh." [23]

Ibn Hajr (may Allāh have mercy on him) added:

> 'al-Nawawi said: the *'ulamā'* said: making images of animate beings is extremely *harām*, and is one of the major sins, because the one who does it is issued with a stern threat, whether the image is something that is treated with disrespect or not. It is haraam to make images whatever the case, whether the image is on a garment, a rug, any kind of coin, a vessel, a wall, or anywhere else. As for any picture that does not contain images of animate creatures, this is not *harām*.'
>
> The general statement regarding images applies to both those that have shadows (three-dimensional images) and those that do not have shadows (two-dimensional images).
>
> This is proven by the *ḥadīth* reported by Aḥmad from 'Alī, who said that the Prophet (ﷺ) said:
>
> "Which of you will go to Madīnah and not leave any idol without breaking it or any picture without blotting it out?" [24]

The Prophet (ﷺ) was always keen to cleanse his house of forbidden pictures, as the following example illustrates:

Under the heading '*Man lām yadkhulu baytan fihi surah* (The one

---

[23] *al-Fath*, [1/382].

[24] *Fath al-Bārī*, [1/348].

who does not enter a house in which there is an image)', al-Bukhārī - may Allāh have mercy on him - narrated the *ḥadīth* of 'Ā'ishah (may Allāh be pleased with her), in which she said that she bought a pillow which had pictures on it. When the Messenger of Allāh (ﷺ) saw it, he stood at the door and did not enter, and she could see from his face that he was upset. She said,

> "O Messenger of Allāh! I repent to Allāh and His Messenger. What have I done wrong?" He said, "What is this pillow?" She said, "I bought it so that you could sit on it and recline on it." The Messenger of Allāh (ﷺ) said: "The makers of these images will be punished on the Day of Resurrection, and they will be told, "Bring to life that which you have created!"And he said: "The house in which there are images, the angels do not enter it." [25]

Some people may say, why have you spoken at such length about this topic? We say: we have entered homes and rooms where we have seen pictures of singers and other people, some of them appearing naked or almost naked, hanging on walls and mirrors and wardrobes, and placed on tables, so that the owners look at them every morning and evening. Some of them even kiss the pictures and have evil thoughts when looking at them! Thus the picture becomes one of the greatest causes of deviation. Anyone who has the eyes to see will understand at least some of the wisdom behind the Islāmic prohibition of making images of animate beings.

We must conclude this discussion by pointing out the following:

---

[25] *Fath al-Bārī*, [1/392].

[i]- Some people say: 'Pictures are everywhere nowadays, even on tins of food, and in books and magazines and pamphlets. If we want to blot out every picture we will waste all out time doing that. What should we do?

We say: try to buy things that have no images in them - if possible. As for the rest, blot out those that are obvious - like pictures on the covers of books, and the rest of the book can be left and used. If it is something that is no longer useful, like a newspaper and the like, remove it from the home. In the case of pictures that it is difficult to erase - like pictures on cans of food, for example - *in sha' Allāh* it is not a sin to leave them as they are, as the scholars have said, because they are things that are difficult to avoid, and the problem is becoming overwhelming.

[ii]- If you have to hang up something to decorate your walls, let it be some scenes of natural views or mosques or things that will not provoke feelings that are *harām.*

The one who hangs up verses of the Qur'ān and so on should pay attention to the fact that the Qur'ān was not revealed to decorate walls, and that it is a kind of disrespect to write verses of the Qur'ān in the shape of a man prostrating or a bird and the like. He should also be careful that people sitting in a gathering do not do things that go against the words of the *āyah* hanging above their heads.

Do not allow smoking in your home

There is enough evidence (for those who are wise) that smoking is *harām* in the words of Allāh:

فَٱلَّذِينَ ءَامَنُوا۟ بِهِۦ وَعَزَّرُوهُ وَنَصَرُوهُ وَٱتَّبَعُوا۟
ٱلنُّورَ ٱلَّذِىٓ أُنزِلَ مَعَهُۥٓ ۙ أُو۟لَـٰٓئِكَ هُمُ ٱلْمُفْلِحُونَ ﴿١٥٧﴾

> **...[Allāh] allows them as lawful *al-tayyibāt* [(i.e., all good and lawful) as regards things, deeds, beliefs, persons, food, etc.] and prohibits them as unlawful *al-khabā'ith* (i.e., all evil and unlawful as regards things, deeds, beliefs, persons, food, etc.)...** [the arabic does match the transation?????]
>
> [*al-A'rāf* (7) : 157]

Allāh has divided food and drink into two categories, not three. There are things that are good and permissible, and there are things that are evil and forbidden. Who could dare to say nowadays that smoking is good, when we know how it stinks and we know how much money is wasted on it and how much physical damage is caused as a result of smoking?

The righteous home should have no lighters or ashtrays, not even those that are given away free as promotional gifts, let alone narghiles ('hubble-bubbles') and the like.

If you are afraid that people may smoke in your home, put up stickers to hint to people that you do not want them to smoke. If you realize that someone wants to commit this sin in front of you, you have to stop him in whatever way is appropriate.

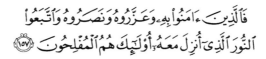

Beware of keeping dogs in your home

One of the habits that have come to us from the *kuffār* is the custom of keeping pet dogs in the home. Many of the people in our society who are following the ways of the *kuffār* bring a dog into their home. They spend money to buy the dog, although the price of a dog is *harām.* [26]

Then they spend money on feeding it and keeping it clean, money which they will be asked about on the Day of Resurrection. Having a dog at home has become a status symbol among many rich people and high-level employees. The dog's saliva is *nājis* (unclean, impure), and the dog licks the members of the household and their vessels. If a dog licks a vessel it must be washed seven times, one of which must be with earth. How about if you realize how much reward is lost by those who keep dogs? The Prophet (ﷺ) said:

> "There is no member of a household where a dog is kept, but their good deeds will be reduced by one *qīrāt* (according to a report narrated by Muslim, by two *qīrāts*) every day, except in the case of a dog kept for hunting, agriculture or herding sheep." [27]

The ban on keeping dogs does not apply to working dogs kept for agriculture, hunting or guarding homes, buildings, livestock, etc. This also includes dogs kept for necessary purposes such as pursuing criminals, sniffing out drugs, and so on, as some schol-

---

[26] According to the *ḥadīth* narrated by Imām Aḥmad, [1/356]; see also *Ṣaḥīḥ al-Jāmi'*, [3071].

[27] Reported by al-Tirmidhī, [1489]; *Ṣaḥīḥ al-Jāmi'*, [5321].

ars have explained.[28]

Jibrīl (peace be upon him) explained to our Prophet Muḥammad (ﷺ) the reason why he could not enter his house at a time they had both agreed upon. The Prophet (ﷺ) said:

> "*Jibrīl* came to me and said: 'I was going to come to you tonight, and nothing stopped me from entering the house you were in except the fact that there was a statue of a man in the house, and a curtain on which there were images, and there was a dog in the house. Tell someone to cut the head off the statue, so it will look like a tree; tell someone to cut up the curtain and make it into two pillows; tell someone to get the dog out of the house.'" So the Messenger of Allāh (ﷺ) did that." [29]

---

[28] *Al-Ta'līq 'ala Sunan al-Tirmidhī*, Shākir edn., [3/267].

[29] Reported by Imām Aḥmad; *Ṣaḥīḥ al-Jāmi'*, [no. 68].

Not going to extremes in decorating the house

In many people's houses nowadays there are all kinds of ornaments and decorations, because of their indulging in leisure and being too attached to this world, and their desire to boast and show off.

When you enter some homes, you are reminded of the words of Ibn 'Abbās:

> 'In Paradise there is nothing of the things of this world except the names.'

We have no room in this brief discussion to go into detail about all the weird and wonderful antiques, decorations, ornaments and engravings with which some homes and palaces are adorned, but we will mention the following:

Allāh says:

وَلَوْلَآ
أَن يَكُونَ ٱلنَّاسُ أُمَّةً وَٰحِدَةً لَّجَعَلْنَا لِمَن يَكْفُرُ بِٱلرَّحْمَٰنِ
لِبُيُوتِهِمْ سُقُفًا مِّن فِضَّةٍ وَمَعَارِجَ عَلَيْهَا يَظْهَرُونَ ﴿٣٣﴾

And were it not that all mankind would have become one community (all disbelievers, desiring worldly life only), We would have provided for those who disbelieve in the Most Beneficent (Allāh), silver roofs for their houses, and elevators (and stairways, etc. of silver), whereby they ascend. And for their houses, doors (of silver), and thrones (of silver) on which they could re-

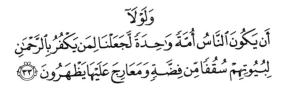

cline, And ornaments of gold...

[*al-Zukhruf* (43) : 33-35]

i.e., were it not for the fact that many ignorant people would think that being given wealth was a sign of being loved by Allāh, which would lead to all of them becoming *kāfirs* for the sake of wealth, Allāh could have given them roofs and staircases and locks of silver and gold from the pleasures of this world, then when they died they would have no *ḥasanah* (good deeds) to their credit, because they had already taken their share of pleasure in this world.[30]

Imām Muslim (may Allāh have mercy on him) reported from 'Ā'ishah (may Allāh be pleased with her) that the Messenger of Allāh (ﷺ) went out on a military campaign, and she took a velvet rug and covered the doorway with it. When he came back and saw the rug, she could see from his face that he was upset. He ripped it down and said,

"Allāh has not commanded us to cover stones and clay with cloth!" [31]

Imām Aḥmad reported the story of Fātimah, when they had made some food and she said to 'Alī (may Allāh be pleased with him),

'Why don't we invite the Messenger of Allāh (peace and blessings of Allāh be upon him) to join us?' So he came, and put his hands on the sides of the door,

---

30 Ibn Kathīr, *Tafsīr al-Qur'ān al-'Aẓīm*, [7/213].

31 *Ṣaḥīḥ Muslim*, [3/1666].

> and saw a *qarām* (a garment made of soft wool, with colourful designs), so he went away. Fātimah said to 'Alī, 'Go and catch up with him, and ask him, 'Why did you go away, O Messenger of Allāh?' [The Prophet (ﷺ)] said, "It is not right for me (according to another report: it is not right for a Prophet) to enter a decorated house." [32]

It was also reported by Abū Dāwūd under the heading: *Rajul yud'ā fa yarā makrūhan* (when a man is invited and sees something disliked). [33]

Under the heading, *Hal yurja' idhā ra'a munkaran fi'l-da'wah?* (should he go back if he sees something objectionable in the invitation?), al-Bukhārī (may Allāh have mercy on him) reported that Ibn 'Umar invited Abū Ayyūb, and he saw a wall-hanging in the house. Ibn 'Umar said,

> 'The women are having their way.' Abū Ayyūb said, 'There are people I was worried about, but you were not one of them! By Allāh, I will never touch your food.' Then he went away.[34]

Imām Aḥmad reported the same story from Sālim ibn 'Abd-Allāh ibn 'Umar, who said:

> 'I got married during my father's lifetime, and my father announced it to the people, and Abū Ayyūb

---

32 Reported by Imām Aḥmad, [5/221]; *Ṣaḥīḥ al-Jāmi'*, [2411].

33 *Sunan Abi Dāwūd*, [3755].

34 *Fath al-Bārī*, [9/249].

> was one of the invited guests. They had covered my house with a striped green cloth, and Abū Ayyūb came and looked at it, then he said, 'Are you covering the walls?' My father felt embarrassed, and said, 'Women are having their way, O Abū Ayyūb.' He said, 'Of all the people I feared would be taken over by the women...' [35]

Al-Ṭabarānī reported from Abū Juḥayfah that the Messenger of Allāh (ﷺ) said:

> "You will have a lot of worldly riches, so much so that you will cover your homes with cloth as the *Ka'bah* is covered. You are better today than you will be on that day." [36]

In brief, what the scholars say about ornamentation and decoration of houses is that it is either *makrūh* or *ḥarām.* [37]

---

[35] *Fath al-Bārī.*

[36] *Ṣaḥīḥ al-Jāmi'*, [3614].

[37] *al-Ādāb al-Shar'iyyah* by Ibn Mufliḥ, [3/421].

THE HOME INSIDE AND OUT

Choosing a good location and design of home.

No doubt the true Muslim pays attention to the choice and design of a home in ways that others do not. With regard to location, for example:

The home should be close to a *masjid.* This has obvious advantages: the call to prayer will remind people of prayer and wake them up for it; living close to the *masjid* will enable men to join the congregational prayers, women to listen to the Qur'ān recitation and *dhikr* over the *masjid*'s loudspeakers, and children to join study-circles for memorization of Qur'ān, and so on.

The home should not be in a building where there are immoral people, or in a compound where *kuffār* live and where there is a mixed swimming pool and so on.

The house should not overlook others or be overlooked; if it is, he should put up curtains and make walls and fences higher.

With regard to design and lay out, for example:

He should pay attention to the matter of segregating men and women when non-*mahrams* come to visit, e.g. separate entrances and sitting areas. If that cannot be done, then use should be made of curtains, screens and so on.

Covering windows, so that neighbours or people in the street will not be able to see who is in the house, especially at night when the lights are on.

The toilets should not be sited in such a way that one faces the qiblah when using them.

Choosing a spacious house with plenty of amenities. This is for a number of reasons:

> "Allāh loves to see the signs of His blessings on His slave." [1]
>
> "There are three elements of happiness and three elements of misery. The elements of happiness are: a righteous wife, who when you see her she pleases you, and when you are absent from her you feel that you can trust her with regard to herself and your wealth; a compliant riding-beast that helps you to keep up with your companions; and a house that is spacious and has plenty of amenities. The elements of misery are: a wife who when you see her you feel upset, she keeps attacking you verbally, and when you are absent from her you do not feel that you can trust her with regard to herself and your wealth; a stubborn riding-beast that if whip it, you get tired, and if you do not whip it, it does not help you to keep up with your compan-

[1] Reported by al-Tirmidhī, no. [2819]. He said: This is a *ḥasan ḥadīth*.

ions; and a house with few amenities." [2]

Paying attention to health-related matters such as ventilation, natural light and so on. These matters depend on financial ability and feasibility.

Choosing the neighbour before the house.

This is a matter which has to be singled out for discussion because of its importance.

Nowadays neighbours have more impact on one another, because houses are closer together and people live together in buildings, apartments and compounds.

The Messenger of Allāh (ﷺ) told us of four causes of happiness, one of which is a righteous neighbour, and four causes of misery, one of which is a bad neighbour. [3]

Because of the seriousness of the latter, the Prophet (ﷺ) used to seek refuge with Allāh from bad neighbours in his *du'ā'*:

«اللهم اني أعوذ بك من جار السوء في
دار المقام فإن جار الدنيا يتحوّل».

"Allāhumma innī a'ūdhu bika min jār al-sū' fi dār il-muqāmah fa inna jār al-bādiyah yatahawwil."

"O Allāh, I seek refuge with You from a bad neigh-

---

[2] Reported by al-Ḥākim, [3/262]; *Ṣaḥīḥ al-Jāmi'*, [no. 3056].

[3] Reported by Abū Na'īm in *al-Ḥilyah*, [8/388]; *Ṣaḥīḥ al-Jāmi'*, [887].

> bour in my permanent home, for the neighbour in the desert [i.e. on a journey] moves on)."

He commanded the Muslims to seek refuge with Allāh from a bad neighbour in a permanent home because the neighbour in the desert will eventually move on. [4]

There is no room here to talk about the influence a bad neighbour may have on a couple and their children, or the kinds of nuisance he can cause, or the misery of living next to him. But applying these *aḥādīth* quoted above to one's own life should be sufficient for the one who is possessed of understanding. Another practical solution is that implemented by some good people who rent neighbouring homes for their families, so as to solve the neighbour problem. This may be an expensive solution, but a good neighbour is priceless.

---

[4] Reported by al-Bukhārī in *al-Adab al-Mufrad*, [no. 117]; *Ṣaḥīḥ al-Jāmi'*, [2967].

Paying attention to necessary repairs in the home, and making sure that the amenities are in good working order.

Among the blessings of Allāh in this modern age are the 'mod cons' that He has bestowed upon us, which make many things easier and save time, such as air-conditioners, fridges, washing-machines and so on. It is wise to have the best quality of appliances that one can afford, without being extravagant or putting oneself under financial strain. We should also be careful to distinguish between useful extras and extravagant additions that have no real value.

Part of caring for the home includes fixing appliances and amenities that break down. Some people neglect these things, and their wives complain about homes crawling with vermin, with overflowing drains and piles of stinking garbage, filled with broken and worn out furniture.

No doubt this is one of the obstacles to happiness in the home, and causes problems in the marriage and health problems. The smart person is the one who hastens to fix these things.

Paying attention to the family's health and safety procedures.

When any member of his family got sick, the Messenger of Allāh (ﷺ) would blow on them and recite *al-Mi'wadhatayn* (last two sūrahs of the Qur'ān). [5]

When one of his family members got sick, he would call for soup, and it would be made for him, then he would tell them to drink it, and he would say,

> "It will strengthen the heart of the one who is grieving and cleanse (heal) the heart of the one who is sick just as any one of you wipes the dirt from her face." [6]

One of the ways of taking safety precautions is:

The Messenger of Allāh (ﷺ) said:

> "When evening comes, keep your children inside, for the shayāṭīn (devils) spread out at that time. Then when an hour of the night has passed, let your children go, lock the doors and mention the name of Allāh, cover your pots and mention the name of Allāh,even if you only place a stick across the top of your vessel, and extinguish your lamps." [7]

---

[5] Reported by Muslim, no. [2192].

[6] Reported by al-Tirmidhī [no. 2039]; *Ṣaḥīḥ al-Jāmi'*, [no. 4646].

[7] Reported by al-Bukhārī, *al-Fath,* [10/88-89].

According to a report narrated by Muslim, he (ﷺ) said:

> "Lock your doors, cover your vessels, extinguish your lamps and tie your knots properly [i.e., cover your jugs properly - in those days they would cover them with a piece of cloth and tie it], for the *Shayṭān* does not open a door that is closed, or uncover something that is covered, or untie a knot that you tie. And the mouse could set the house on fire (i.e. it could pull out the wick of the lamp and set the house on fire)." [8]

The Prophet (ﷺ) said:

> "Do not leave fires lit in your houses when you go to sleep." [9]

And Allāh knows best. May Allāh bless our Prophet Muḥammad (ﷺ).

---

[8] Reported by Imām Aḥmad in *al-Musnad*, [3/103]; *Ṣaḥīḥ al-Jāmi'*, [1080].

[9] Reported by al-Bukhārī, *al-Fath*, [11/85].

BIOGRAPHICAL NOTES

'Ā'ISHAH: bint Abū Bakr *as-Ṣiddīq*, the Mother of the Believers and most beloved wife of the Prophet (ﷺ). She reported many *aḥādīth* from the Prophet and many Companions and Successors reported from her. She died in the year 58H.

'ABDULLĀH BIN 'ABBĀS: bin 'Abdul-Muṭṭalib bin Hāshim bin 'Abd Munāf al-Qurashī al-Hāshimī, the cousin of the Prophet (ﷺ) and the interpreter of the Qur'ān. He was born three years before the *Hijrah* and was called the 'Ocean of knowledge' due to his vast knowledge. He took part in the *Jihād* in North Africa in the year 27H and died in the year 68H.

'ABDULLĀH BIN 'AMR: bin al-'Ās bin Wā'il bin Hāshim bin Su'ayd bin Sa'd bin Sahm as-Sahmī. He and his father were Companions. He was literate and attained permission from the Prophet (ﷺ) to write everything he said. He died in the year 65H.

'ABDULLĀH ABŪ JĀBIR: bin 'Amr bin Ḥazzām bin Thalabah al-Anṣārī al-Khazrajī as-Sulamī, amongst those who gave the pledge of *'Uqbah*. He witnessed *Badr* and was martyred at *Uḥud*.

'ABDULLĀH BIN MAS'ŪD: bin Ghāfil bin Ḥabīb al-Hadhlī Abū 'Abdur-Raḥmān. One of the scholars amongst the Companions and he witnessed *Badr* and the following battles. He had many virtues and died in the year 32H.

'ABDULLĀH BIN 'UMAR: bin al-Khaṭṭāb al-'Adawī, Abū 'Abdur-Raḥmān, the noble Companion and scholar. He reported many *aḥādīth* from the Messenger (ﷺ) and died in the year 73H.

'ABDUR-RAḤMĀN BIN AUF: bin Awf bin Abd Awf bin al-Ḥārith al-Qurashī az-Zuhrī, Abū Muḥammad, one of the ten promised Paradise. He migrated to Abysinnia on both occasions and witnessed every battle with the Prophet (ﷺ). He was very rich and very generous when giving in the Way of Allāh. He died in the year 32H.

ABŪ BAKR AS-ṢIDDĪQ: 'Abdullāh bin 'Uthmān bin Āmir al-Qurashī. The first *Khalīfah* of the Messenger (ﷺ), his companion in the cave, his closest friend and one of the ten promised Paradise. He was the first man to accept Islām and died in the year 13H.

ABŪ AD-DARDĀ': Uwaymir bin Mālik bin Zayd bin Qays al-Khazrajī al-Anṣārī. There is a difference of opinion concerning his name. He accepted Islām on the day of *Badr* and witnessed *Uḥud*. He was from the Legal Jurists and ascetics of the Companions. He died in the year 32H.

ABŪ DHARR AL-GHIFĀRĪ: Jundub bin Junādah bin Sakn, he was of those who accepted Islām early on but delayed his migration and hence did not witness *Badr*. His virtues are many and he died in the year 32H.

ABŪ HURAYRAH: 'Abdur-Raḥmān bin Ṣakhr ad-Dusī. His name is greatly differed over. He accepted Islām in the year 7H and reported the most ḥadīth from the Prophet (ﷺ). He died in the year 59H.

ABŪ MŪSĀ AL-ASH'ARĪ: 'Abdullāh bin Qays bin Salīm. He had a beautiful recitation and was one of the scholars amongst the Companions. He died in the year 42H or 44H.

ABŪ SA'ĪD AL-KHUDRĪ: Sa'd bin Mālik bin Sinān bin 'Ubaid al-

Anṣārī al-Khazrajī. He and his father were both Companions and he witnessed all the battles that followed *Uḥud.* He was one of the scholars amongst the Companions and reported many *aḥādīth* from the Messenger (ﷺ). He died in the year 74H.

ABŪ 'UBAIDAH BIN AL-JARRĀḤ: 'Āmir bin 'Abdullāh bin al-Jarrāḥ bin Hilāl al-Qurashī al-Fahrī, one of the ten promised Paradise. He accepted Islām early on and witnessed the battle of *Badr* and the following battles. He is the trustworthy one of this nation and died as a martyr due to a plague in the year 18H at the age of fifty-eight.

'ADĪ BIN ḤĀTIM: bin 'Abdullāh bin Sa'd bin al-Ḥashraj bin 'Amr al-Qays at-Ṭā'ī, Abu Ṭarīf. He was a Christian who accepted Islām and witnessed the battles of *al-Jamal*, *Ṣiffīn* and *an-Nahrawān* with 'Alī. He died in the year 68H.

Al-'AlĀ' BIN AL-KHAḌRAMĪ: al-Khazrajī. His supplications would be answered and he died in the year 21H.

'ALĪ BIN ABĪ ṬĀLIB: bin 'Abdul-Muṭṭalib bin Hāshim al-Qurashī al-Hāshimī, the fourth Rightly Guided *Khalīfah* and one of ten promised Paradise. He accepted Islām at the age of thirteen and was famous for his chivalry, bravery and knowledge. He married Fāṭimah, the daughter of the Prophet (ﷺ) and was martyred in the year 40H.

'AMR BIN AL-'ĀS: bin Wā'il al-Qurashī as-Sahmī. He accepted Islām during the year of *Ḥudaybiyyah* and was the one who conquered Egypt. He died in the year 43H.

ANAS BIN MĀLIK: bin an-Naḍar bin Ḍamḍam al-Anṣārī al-Khazrajī, the servant of the Messenger (ﷺ). He witnessed *Badr* but was not of age to actually participate. He died in the year 93H.

AL-BARĀ'A BIN MĀLIK: bin an-Naḍr al-Anṣārī. He witnessed *Uḥud* and gave the pledge of allegiance under the tree. He was martyred in the year 20H on the Day of *Tustor*.

'IMRĀN BIN ḤUSAIN: al-Khuzā'ī al-Ka'bī Abū Nujaid. He accepted Islām during the year of *Khaybar* and reported some *aḥādīth* from the Prophet (ﷺ). He died in the year 52H.

JĀBIR BIN 'ABDULLĀH: bin 'Amr bin Ḥarrām al-Anṣārī as-Sulamī, he witnessed the second pledge at *'Uqbah* while he was still a child. It is said that he witnessed *Badr* and *Uḥud* and he reported many *aḥādīth* from the Messenger (ﷺ). He died in the year 74H.

KHĀLID BIN AL-WALĪD: bin al-Mughīrah al-Makhzūmī al-Qurashī Abū Sulaymān. He was a great warrior and military leader and was given the nickname, 'Sword of Allāh.' He died in the year 21H.

KHUBAIB BIN 'ADĪ: bin Mālik bin 'Āmir al-Awsī al-Anṣārī. He witnessed *Badr* and was martyred during the lifetime of the Prophet (ﷺ) when he was captured by the polytheists in Mecca.

MU'ĀDH BIN JABAL: bin 'Amr bin Aws al-Anṣārī al-Khazrajī, Abū 'Abdur-Raḥmān, one of the foremost Companions known for his knowledge of legal rulings and the Qur'ān. He was present at the pledge of *'Uqbah* and witnessed *Badr* and the following battles and was martyred due to a plague in the year 17H or 18H.

MU'ĀWIYAH: bin Abū Sufyān bin Ṣakhr bin Ḥarb bin Umayyah bin 'Abd Shams al-Qurashī al-Amawī. He accepted Islām in the year of the Conquest and witnessed *Ḥunain* and *al-Yamāmah*. He was one of the scribes who would write the revelation and died in the year 60H.

AL-MUGHĪRAH BIN SHU'BAH: bin Abū 'Āmir bin Mas'ūd ath-Thaqafī, Abū 'Abdullāh. He witnessed *Hudaybiyyah*, *al-Yamāmah* and the conquests of Syria and Iraq. He died in the year 50H.

QATĀDAH: ibn an-Nu'mān bin Zayd al-Anṣārī al-Awsī, Abū 'Amr, he witnessed the pledge of *'Uqbah*, *Badr* and every other battle that the Prophet (ﷺ) fought. He died in the year 23H.

SA'D BIN ABĪ WAQQĀS: Sa'd bin Mālik bin Ahīb bin 'Abd Munāf al-Qurashī az-Zuhrī Abū Isḥāq bin Abī Waqqās. One of the ten who were promised Paradise and one whose supplications were answered. He was the last of the ten to pass away in the year 55H.

SA'ĪD BIN ZAYD: bin 'Amr al-Adawī al-Qurashī. He witnessed all the battles except for *Badr* and was one of the ten promised Paradise. He died in the year 51H.

SAFĪNAH: He was a Persian slave who was bought by Umm Salamah and subsequently freed. He then devoted himself to serving the Prophet (ﷺ).

SALMĀN: al-Fārisī Abū 'Abdullāh, the servant of the Messenger (ﷺ). The first battle he witnessed was *al-Khandaq* and he was present at all following battles. He died in the year 36H.

SHADDĀD BIN AWS: bin Thābit al-Anṣārī al-Khazrajī, Abū Ya'lā. He was famous for his knowledge and wisdom and died in the year 58H.

ṬALḤAH: bin 'Ubaydullāh bin 'Uthmān bin 'Amr al-Qurashī, Abū Muḥammad, one of the ten promised Paradise. He witnessed *Uḥud* and the following battles. He died in the year 36H.

'UMAR BIN AL-KHAṬṬĀB: Abū Ḥafs 'Umar bin al-Khaṭṭāb bin Nufayl al-Qurashī al-'Adawī, the second Rightly Guided *Khalīfah* and one of the ten promised Paradise. He accepted Islām five years before the *Hijrah* and his acceptance was a great victory for the Muslims. He witnessed every battle that the Prophet (ﷺ) witnessed. He was martyred in the year 23H.

'UTHMĀN BIN 'AFFĀN: *Dhu an-Nurayn* 'Uthmān bin 'Affān bin Abū al-'Ās bin Umayyah al-Qurashī al-Amawī, the third Rightly Guided *Khalīfah* and one of the ten promised Paradise. He was known for his generosity and freely giving in the Way of Allāh. He was married to two daughters of the Prophet (ﷺ), Ruqayyah and after her death, Umm Kulthūm. He was martyred in the year 35H.

AZ-ZUBAIR: bin al-Awām bin Khuwaylid bin Asad al-Qurashī al-Asadī, Abū 'Abdullāh. He migrated to Abysinnia on both the migrations there and accompanied the Messenger on all his military expeditions. He was one of the ten promised Paradise and died in the year 36H.

Others

'ABD AL-'AZĪZ IBN BAZ: 'Abdul-'Azīz ibn Baz was the leading scholar and was the president of the board of leading scholars in Saudi Arabia. He has been blind since his youth but well known for his great memory. He taught for many years and was also the Chancellor of the Islāmic University of Medīnah. He died in the year 1420H, the end of a blessed life lasting eighty-nine years. His death is indeed a great loss to the Islāmic World.

'ABD-AL-MĀLIK BIN MARWĀN: bin al-Ḥakam, Abū al-Walīd, the Leader of the Believers. He was a Legal Jurist and possessed knowledge of the religion. He died in the year 86H.

AL-AWZĀ'Ī: 'Abdur-Raḥmān bin 'Amr bin Muḥammad, Abū 'Amr, one of the great scholars of his time. He was well versed in ḥadīth, *fiqh* and the military expeditions undertaken by the Prophet (ﷺ). The Muslims have agreed as to his excellence and being an *Imām*. His *fiqh* dominated Spain for a time and he died in the year 158H.

ABŪ DĀWŪD: Sulaymān bin al-Ash'ath bin Isḥāq bin Bashīr, Abū Dāwūd as-Sijistānī, the *Imām*, *Ḥāfiẓ* and author of the famous *Sunan*. He died in the year 275H.

ABŪ NU'AYM: The great *Ḥāfiẓ* and *Muḥaddith* of his age, Aḥmad bin 'Abdullāh bin Aḥmad bin Isḥāq bin Mūsā bin Mahrān al-Asbahānī *as-Ṣūfīs*. He died in the year 430H at the age of ninety-four.

ABŪ YA'LA, AḤMAD BIN 'ALĪ: *Al-Ḥāfiẓ* Aḥmad bin 'Alī bin Al-Muthanna bin Yaḥya bin 'Īsa bin Ḥilal At-Tamimī was born in Shawwal, 210 H.He authored *Al-Musnad Al-Kabir* and was considered as the *Muḥaddith* of Al-Jazira. He was truthful, trustworthy, tolerant and religious. As-Sam'anī said, 'I heard Ismaiil bin Muḥammad bin Al-Faḍl *Al-Ḥāfiẓ* say: 'I read the *Musnad* of Al-'Adani, the *Musnad* of Ibn Mani' and other *Masānid*, which are like rivers, but the *Musnad* of Abū Ya'la is like the sea into which all the rivers flow." Abū Ya'la died in the year 307 H.

AḤMAD: bin Muḥammad bin Ḥanbal bin Hilāl ash-Shaybānī, Abū 'Abdullāh, the *Imām* of the *Sunnah* and author of the famous *Musnad.* He was known for his knowledge of ḥadīth, *fiqh*, and his *taqwā* and asceticism. He died in the year 241H.

AL-BAYHAQĪ: Aḥmad bin al-Ḥusayn bin 'Alī bin 'Abdullah bin Mūsā, Abū Bakr al-Bayhaqī al-Naysaburī al-Khusrawjirdī al-Shāfi'i. The *Imām*, *Ḥāfiẓ*, ascetic and one of the main proponents of the al-Shāfi'i school. He studied under a host of the leading scholars of his time and a large group took from him. His works are marked by their meticulousness and reliability, amongst them are: *as-Sunan al-Kubrā, Ma'rifah as-Sunan wal Athār, al-Asmā'was Sifāt, al-I'tiqād, Dala'il an-Nubuwwah* and *Shu'ab al-Imān.*

BAKR ABŪ ZAID: Bakr Abū Zaid is a contemporary scholar living in Saudi Arabia. Highly respected for his knowledge, he has written extensively on ibn al-Qayyim. He is currently a member of the board of leading scholars in Saudi Arabia.

AL-BAZZĀR, AḤMAD BIN 'AMR: Abū Bakr, Aḥmad bin 'Amr bin 'Abdul-Khāliq Al-Basrī was one of the eminent and learned *Ḥadīth* scholars who had attained the rank of *Ḥāfiẓ* in the memorization of *Ḥadīth*. He authored two books on *Ḥadīth* which are *Al-Musnad Al-Kabir* and *Al-'Ilal*. He studied under At-Tabarānī and others. Al-Bazzār died in 292 H.

BUKHĀRĪ: Muḥammad bin Ismā'īl bin Ibrāhīm bin al-Mughīrah, Abū 'Abdullāh. He was born in the year 194H and became one of the *Imāms* of ḥadīth and was nicknamed 'The Leader of the Believers in Ḥadīth.' He died in the year 256H.

AD-DĀRIMĪ, 'ABDULLĀH BIN 'ABDUR-RAḤMĀN: Abū Muḥamrnad, 'Abdullāh bin 'Abdur-Raḥmān bin Al-Faḍl bin Bahram At-Tamimī Ad-Dārimī As-Samarqandī was born in the year 181 H. He was acelebrated *Imām*, *Ḥāfiẓ* and Shaikh-ul-Islām of Samarqand and the author of *Al-Musnad Al- 'Aali*. He heard *Ḥadīth* at Al-Haramain, Khurasan, Ash-Sham, Iraq and Egypt. Muslim, Abū Dāwūd, At-Tirmidhī, An-Nasā'i and others transmitted Ḥadīth from him. He was described to be very intelligent and very virtuous and was considered to be an exemplary person in piousness, patience, hardwork, worship and abstinence. Ad-Dārimī died on 8th Dhul-Hijja 255H.

AD-DĀRUQUTNĪ: 'Alī bin Umar bin Ahmad, the *Imām* of his era in *ḥadīth*, knowledge of the defects of *aḥādīth* and author of the famous *Sunan*. He was well versed in the various recitations of the Qur'ān, *fiqh*, language and poetry. He died in the year 385H.

AD-DAHHĀK: bin Muzāhim al-Hilālī, Abū al-Qāsim al-Khurasānī, the *Imām* of *tafsīr*. He was trustworthy and precise and a student of Sa'īd bin Jubair. He died in the year 105H.

Al-ḤAṢAN AL-BAṢRĪ: Al-Ḥasan bin Abū al-Ḥasan al-Anṣārī. He was trustworthy and precise, noble and famous. He was a great scholar and narrated many *aḥādīth*. He died in the year 110H close to the age of ninety.

AL-ḤARITH BIN ABŪ USĀMA: Imām Abū Muhammad, Al-Ḥarith bin Abū Usāma Muhammad bin Dahir At-Tamīmī Al-Baghdādī was a *Ḥāfiẓ* and authored *Al-Musnad* which he did not arrange. Ibrāhīm Al-Harbī and Abū Hātim verified him as reliable, and Ad-Daraqutnī said, ṇHe is truthful.ī Al-Ḥarith was born in 186 H. And died on the day of 'Arafa 282 H.

IBN ABĪ SHAYBAH, ABŪBAKR: Abū Bakr 'Abdullāh bin Muḥammad bin Abī Shaybah Ibrāhīm bin 'Uthmān bin Hawasī Al-'Ansī (by clientship) was a unique *Ḥāfiẓ*. He authored *Al-Musnad wal-Musannaf* and other books. He was a leader in the knowledge of Ḥadīth and Abū Zur'ā, Al-Bukhārī, Muslim, Abu Dāwud and Khalaf narrated it from him. Abū Bakr died in Muharram, 235 H.

IBN KHUZAYMAH, MUḤAMMAD BIN ISHĀQ: Ibn Khuzaymah, Muhammad bin Ishāq was born in 223 H. In Nishapur. He was considered as a Shaikh-ul-lslām (the most learned 'Alim of Islām) and one of the eminent and senior *Ḥāfiẓ*. He was the Imām and *Ḥāfiẓ* of Khurasān during his time. He also authored more than 140 books. Ibn Khuzaymah died in Nishapur in 311 H.

IBN ḤIBBĀN: Abū Ḥātim Muḥammad ibn Ḥibbān al-Tamīmī al-Bustī, the *Ḥāfiẓ*, *Mujtahid* and author of the famous *Ṣaḥīḥ ibn Ḥibbān*. He died in the year 354H.

IBN KATHĪR: 'Imād al-Dīn Ibn Kathīr, was a scholars of *tafsīr*, language, history and *ḥadīth*. He was born in Jandal in a province of Basrah and then moved to Damasus where he died. His works works include the famous commentary of the Qur'ān, entitled *Tafsīr al-Qur'ān al-'Aẓīm*.

HĀSAN IBN 'ATTIYYA: Originally from Basra, he was among the first generation after the companions. Many of al-Awzā'ī's hadith include him in their transmission chains.

IBN ABŪ AD-DUNYA, 'ABDULLĀH BIN MUHAMMAD BIN 'UBAID: Abū Bakr, 'Abdullāh bin Muḥammad bin 'Ubaid bin Sufyān bin Abū Ad-Dunya Al-Qurashi Al-Baghdādī, the freed slave of Banu 'Umaiyah, was born in 208 H. He was a *Muḥaddith* and truthful 'Alim. He wrote some books and educated more than one of the caliphs sons like Al-Mu'tadid. Ibn Abu Ad-Dunya died in Jumada Al-Ula, 281 H.

IBN QUDĀMAH: Muwaffaq al-Dīn 'Abdullāh ibn Muḥammad ibn Qudāmah was from Palestine. He came from a family that is known for its great scholarship in the Hanbali school of fiqh, Ibn Qudāmah wrote one of the greatest works in *fiqh*, *al-Mugni*. He died in the year of 620H.

IBN 'UTHAYMĪN: Muḥammad ibn Sāliḥ Ibn 'Uthaymīn was born in Unayzah and was one of the leading scholars in Saudi Arabia in his time. He studied with scholars such as 'Abdur-Raḥmān as-Sādi and Muḥammad Amīn ash-Shanqīṭī. He is respected as one of the more well-grounded jurist until present time. He died in the year 1421H.

AL-KHATTABBĪ: Abū Sulaymān Hamād ibn Muḥammad al-Khattabbī came from Bust in Afghanistan. He travelled widely in search of religious knowledge, to Makkah, Basra, Baghdad and Naisaboor. He wrote an excellent commentary on Abū Dāwūd's Sunan, *'Mālim as-Sunnah'*. This work has been quoted and used by all the major commentators who came afterwards.

AL-MUNĀWĪ 'ABDUR-RAUF: Al-Munāwī was a shafi'ī scholar who lived in Cairo. He produced a number of works, perhaps the most important being related to hadith. Through lack of food and sleep, he became ill and weak, leading up to his death 1031H.

MĀLIK BIN ANAS: ibn Mālik ibn Abū 'Amr al-Asbāhī. The *Imām* of Madīnah in his time, one of the great *Imāms* of Islām and author of the famous *Muwattā*. His virtues are many and the scholar's praise of him is abundant. He died in the year 179H.

MUJĀHID: Mujāhid ibn Jabar. He was born in the year 21A.H, during caliphate of 'Umar ibn Khattāb. He was the youngest of Ibn 'Abbās's major student in *tafsīr*. Mujāhid stated, 'I read the Qur'ān to Ibn 'Abbās three times and stopped after every verse asking, 'Concerning what and when was that verse revealed." Many of his reports may be found in Ṣaḥīḥ al-Bukhārī. He died in Makkah in the year 104A.H., while he was in the act of prostration.

MUSLIM: bin al-Ḥajjāj bin Muslim al-Qushayrī, Abū al-Ḥusain an-Naisābūrī, the *Ḥāfiẓ* and one of the great *Imāms* of this nation. He is the author of the Ṣaḥīḥ which is the most authentic book of ḥadīth after Bukhārī. He died in the year 261H.

AN-NASĀ'Ī: Aba 'Abdur-Raḥmān Aḥmad bin Shu'ayb bin 'Ali al-Khurasanī The author of the famous *Sunan*, the *mujaḥid* and *Ḥāfiẓ*. He was known for his strictness in grading ḥadīth narrators.

AL-QADĪ: Abu Ya'la Muḥammad bin al-Ḥasan bin al-Farrā' al-Baghdādī, the *Imām* of the Ḥanbalī *madhab* in his time without any contention. He accompanied *Shaykh* ibn Ḥamid until the latter died in 403H as well as accompanying al-Husayn bin al-Baghdādī and others. A large group of scholars studied under him. From amongst his works are, *al-'Uddah fī Usul al-Fiqh, Ibsal at-Ta'wilāt, al-Imān, al-'Aqīdah, Kitāb ar-Riwāyatayn wa al-Wajhayn, at-Ta'liq al-Kubrā fī al-Fiqh.*

AS-SĀ'DI 'ABDUR-RAḤMĀN: Born in 'Unayzah, Saudi Arabia. His teachers included Uthmān al-Qādhī and Muhammad al-Shanqītī. Over ten of his books have been beneficial commentary on the Qur'ān, '*Taysīr al-Karīm al-Rahmān*.' He died in the Year 1376H.

SA'ĪD BIN MANSŪR: Sa'īd bin Mansūr bin Shu'ba Al-Marwazī or At-Taliqanī then Al-Balkhī lived near Makkah. He authored the book As-Sunan. Imām Aḥmad bin Hanbal praised him immensely. Harb Al-Karmanī said, 'He (Sa'īd) dictated to me about ten thousand ḥadīth from his memory.' Safid bin Mansūr died in Makkah in Ramadān 227 H, while in his nineties.

SA'ĪD BIN AL-MUSAYYAB: bin Hazn, Abū Muḥammad. He excelled in ḥadīth and *fiqh*, and was known for his worship and asceticism. He was one of the 'seven Legal Jurists' of Madīnah and Imaam Aḥmad regarded him to be the most virtuous of the Successors. He was trustworthy and precise and narrated many *aḥadīth*. He died in the year 94H.

SAḤL BIN 'ABDULLĀH: bin Yunus Abū Muḥammad at-Tustorī, one of the *Sūfī* scholars. He died in the year 283H.

ASH-SHĀFI'Ī: Muḥammad bin Idrīs bin al-'Abbās bin Shāfi'ī al-Hāshimī al-Qurashī, Abū 'Abdullāh, the *Mujaddid* of his era and one of the great *Imāms* of this nation. He died in the year 204H.

SUFYĀN ATH-THAWRĪ: bin Sa'īd bin Masrūq, Abū 'Abdullāh ath-Thawrī, one of the great *Imāms* and worshippers of this nation. He was titled 'the Leader of Believers in ḥadīth' and was well versed in *tafsīr*. He was the teacher of Abū Hanīfah and Mālik amongst others and died in the year 161H.

SHAYṬĀN: Also called *Iblīs*. He is a Jinn and the enemy of mankind, devoted to leading them astray in any way that he can. The word Shayṭān is derived from the verb *shaṭana* which means to be distant, and indeed Shayṭān is distant from all good.

AL-TABĀRĪ ABŪ JAFAR MUḤAMMAD IBN JARĪR: Al-Tabārī was a great historian, an eminent jurist of the rank of *mujahid*, and an outstanding commentator on the Qur'ān. His Qur'ānic commentary

'Jāmi' al-bayān fi Tawil Ayi al-Qur'ān', is considered by many to be the greatest commentary available that is based on the tradition of the early generations. He died in the year of 310H.

AT-TABARĀNĪ, SULAIMĀN BIN AḤMAD: Abūl-Qāsim, Sulaimān bin Ahmad bin Ayyūb bin Mutair Al-LakhmīAt-Tabarānī was born in 260 H. in Tabariya As-Sham. He was an authoritative Imām and narrated Ḥadīth from more than one thousand scholars. He left Ash-Sham to acquire the knowledge of Ḥadīth and spent thirty-three years of travelling in its pursuance. He authored many interesting and amusing books, among them are *Al-Mu'jam Al-Kabir*, *Al-Mu'jam Al-Awsat*, and *Al-Mu'jam As-Saghir*. At-Tabarānī lived in Asfahān and died there on 27th Dhul-Qa'da, 360 H.

AT-TIRMIDHĪ: Muḥammad bin 'Īsā bin Sawrah bin Mūsā bin ad-Ḍaḥḥāk as-Sulamī at-Tirmidhī, the *Imām*, *Ḥāfiẓ* and the author of the famous *Sunan*. He was trustworthy and precise and one of the students of Bukhārī. He died in the year 279H.

INDEX OF ARABIC WORDS

AWLIYĀ': plural of *walī*; friend, ally, loyal companion. From the word *wilāyah* meaning loyalty and closeness, the opposite of enmity.

'AYY: withholding the tongue from speaking, carefully considering each word before it is said.

BARZAKH: barrier, isthmus, A barrier that is erected between the deceased and this life preventing him from returning and a generic reference to the life that commences after death.

BAYĀN: Speech, clarification, discourse. It is of two types: the first whereby the intended meaning is expressed clearly, whatever language it may be in, this category is not regarded as magic; the second whereby the intended meaning is expressed in eloquent, cleverly doctored phrases based upon specific rules such that one listening takes pleasure in hearing the words and they affect his very heart. This category is what has been likened to magic as it captivates and beguiles the heart and overcomes the soul to the point that the face of reality could be transformed to illusion and the one captivated perceive only that which the speaker wants him to perceive. This category can be used in a commendable fashion and in a blameworthy fashion. As for the commendable form, it is to direct the person towards the truth and use these methods to aid the truth. As for the blameworthy form, it is to direct the person towards falsehood or envelop him in confusion such that the truth is seen as falsehood and falsehood as truth. This is completely blameworthy and has been likened to that which is completely blameworthy - magic

BIDʿAH: innovation, that which is newly introduced into the religion of Allāh.

ḌAʿĪF: weak; the ḥadīth that is neither ṣaḥīḥ nor ḥasan because it fails to meet one of their requirements. It is of varying degrees of severity, the most severe of which being mauḍūʿ, fabricated.

DHAWQ: taste, perceptivity, technically referring to spiritual experience, *dhawq* is a more temporary state of *wajd*. One may receive some forms of inspiration in the heart as a result of these states however this inspiration should always be compared to the Book and Sunnah to ascertain its correctness.

DHIKR: remembrance, recollection, technically referring the remembrance of Allāh.

DUʿĀ: supplication, invocation, it is an action of worship that may only be directed to Allāh. It is of two types, supplication through worship (*duʿā ʿibādah*) and supplication of request (*duʿā masʾalah*). The first type of *duʿā* can be understood when one understands that every act of worship is done with the unstated plea that Allāh accept that action of worship and the desire to draw closer to him; and hence attain His pleasure. Hence every action of worship is a type of request to Allāh. The second type of *duʿā* is whereby one explicitly asks his Lord of something such as 'O Allāh! Grant me good in this world and the Hereafter.' The second type includes the first type and the first type necessitates the second type.

ḤADĪTH: A text attributed to the Prophet (ﷺ) describing his actions, words, descriptions and tacit approvals. It consists of two portions, the body of the text (*matn*) and the *isnād*.

Rarely the term is also used to refer to a text attributed to a Companion or a *Tābi'ī*.

ḤĀFIẒ: pl. *Ḥuffāẓ*. Ḥadīth Master, commonly referred to one who has memorised at least 100000 ḥadīths.

ḤASAN: good, fair. A ḥadīth whose *isnād* is continuously linked of just, morally upright narrators but whose precision (*ḍabṭ*) falls short of the requirements of the ṣaḥīḥ ḥadīth; containing no irregularity (*shādh*) and no hidden defect (*'illah*). A ḥadīth can be ḥasan in and of itself, or contain a defect but still be ruled to be so due to supporting evidences.

ḤAYĀ': modesty, derived from the word *ḥayāt*, or life because it is through modesty that the heart is granted life and it is through the absence of modesty that it dies. It is a state that arises through the servant being aware that Allāh is watching him, having love, fear and awe of Him and thinking little of himself. Al-Junayd said, '*al-Ḥayā'* is to recognise the bounties of Allāh and then to recognise ones own shortcomings. Through this a state is engendered which is termed *al-Ḥayā'*, the reality of which is that it is a mannerism that prevents one from committing vile actions and from being lax in fulfilling the rights of Allāh.'

ḤUDŪD: limits, boundaries. The limits ordained by Allāh, prescribed punishments.

ḤULŪL WA-L-ITTIḤĀD: incarnation and unification, the settling of a superior faculty upon a support.

IḤSĀN: beneficence, excellence. To worship Allāh as if one is seeing Him, and knowing that even though one sees Him not, He sees the servant.

IKHLĀṢ: sincerity, to strip oneself of worshiping any besides Allāh such that everything one does is performed only to draw closer to Him and for His pleasure. It is to purify ones actions from any but the Creator having a share in them, from any defect or self-desire. The one who has true *ikhlāṣ* (*mukhliṣ*) will be free of *riyā'*.

'ILM: knowledge.

ĪMĀN: The firm belief, complete acknowledgement and acceptance of all that Allāh and His Messenger have commanded to have faith in, submitting to it both inwardly and outwardly. It is the acceptance and belief of the heart that includes the actions of the heart and body, therefore it encompasses the establishment of the whole religion. This is why the Imāms and Salaf used to say, 'Faith is the statement of the heart and tongue, action of the heart, tongue and limbs.' Hence it comprises statement, action and belief, it increases through obedience and decreases through disobedience. It includes the beliefs of faith, its morals and manners and the actions demanded by it.

ISLĀM: submission, submitting to the will of Allāh through following His law as revealed upon the tongue of the Messenger (ﷺ).

ISNĀD: support. The chain of authorities on which a narration is based, linking the end narrator of a narration to the one it is attributed to, be it the Prophet (ﷺ) or anyone else, narrator by narrator.

ISTIDRĀJ: gradually leading to a desired conclusion. Technically refers to Allāh gradually leading one who displays ingratitude to His favours to his destruction as a befitting recompense. Some of the Salaf would say, 'When you see Allāh bestowing His blessings upon you, one after the other, and you are steadfast in disobeying Him, then beware for this is *istidrāj* by which He gradually leads you to destruction.'

ITTIBĀ': following, technically referring to following the Sunnah of the Prophet (ﷺ).

'IYĀFAH: the practice of divination through frightening birds, the sounds they make and the directions in which they fly.

JĀHILIYYAH: Pre-Islāmic Ignorance. Technically this refers to the condition of a people before the guidance of Allāh reaches them, or the state of a people that prevents them from accepting the guidance of Allāh.

JAHL: ignorance.

KALĀM: speech, discourse. Technically used to refer to dialectics and scholastic theology.

KHALAF: successors. A reference to those who followed a path other than the path of the Salaf.

KHALĪFAH: pl. *khulafā'*. Successor, representative. The Successors of the Prophet (ﷺ), head of the Islāmic state. Also called *Amīr al-Mu'minīn* or Leader of the Believers.

KHUSHŪ': submissiveness, humility.

KUFR: denial, rejection, hiding, technically referring to disbelief. It can be major (removing a person from the fold of Islām) or minor (not removing a person from the fold of Islām).

MAJHŪL: unknown. A reference to a narrator from whom only one narrator narrates (*majhūl al-'ain*) or whose state of precision (*ḍabṭ*) is unknown (*majhūl al-ḥāl*), such a narrator makes the *isnād ḍa'īf*.

MA'RIFAH: gnosis. Knowledge that is acted upon by the one who knows, the Gnostic of Allāh is one who has knowledge of Allāh, the path that leads to Allāh and the pitfalls of that path. He is one who knows Allāh, His Names, Attributes and Actions and then displays *ṣidq* and *ikhlāṣ* towards Allāh in all things. He works towards removing all despicable morals and mannerisms and has *ṣabr* in all of this.

MATRŪK: abandoned. A narrator who is accused of lying, or makes many mistakes, or makes mistakes in aḥādith that are agreed upon, or narrates from famous narrators that which those narrators do not know.

MUDALLIS: one who does *tadlīs*

Munqaṭiʿ: that ḥadīth from which the narrator just before the Companion has been omitted from its *isnād*.

MURĀQABAH: self-inspection. The servant having the sure knowledge that Allāh sees him in all circumstances and knows all that he is doing, as such the he does his utmost not to fall into the prohibited matters and to correct his own failings.

MURSAL: disconnected. A ḥadīth whereby a *Tābiʿī* narrates directly from the Prophet (ﷺ) without mentioning the Companion. In the view of the majority of Scholars it is a subcategory of ḍaʿīf.

QADR: Divine Decree and Destiny.

QUR'ĀN: The actual Word of Allāh revealed to the Prophet (ﷺ) in the Arabic language through the medium of the Angel Gabriel and the greatest miracle bestowed him. It consists of 114 chapters commencing with al-Fātiḥah and ending with an-Nās.

RIYĀ': showing off, ostentation, an example of which lies in person beautifying actions of worship because he knows people are watching.

RUQYĀ: recitation used to cure an illness or disease. It can only be done in the Arabic tongue, in words whose meaning is understood, using verses of the Qur'ān or supplications of the Prophet combined with the belief that it is only Allāh who in reality gives the cure.

ṢABR: patience and steadfastness, the restraint of ones self to that which is dictated by the divine law. It is of three levels, steadfastness in the obedience of Allāh, steadfastness in avoiding the prohibited matters and patience at the onset of calamity. *Ikhlāṣ* can never be complete without *ṣidq* and *ṣidq* can never be complete without *ikhlāṣ* and the two can never be complete without *ṣabr*. The person is patient through Allāh, i.e. seeking His aid Alone; for Allāh, i.e. arising out of love for Him and the desire to draw close to Him; and with Allāh, i.e. doing only that which He wills.

ṢAḤĀBAH: The Companions of the Prophet (ﷺ), those who saw him, believed in him and died upon that belief.

ṢĀḤĪḤ: correct, authentic. A ḥadith which has a continuously linked *isnād*, of just, morally upright and precise narrators; containing no irregularity (*shādh*) or hidden defect (*ʿillah*). Hence five conditions have to be met: the *isnād* being continuously linked; the justice (*ʿadl*) of the narrator; the precision (*ḍabṭ*) of the narrator; its not being *shādh*; and its not containing an *ʿillah*. The ḥadīth can be ṣaḥīḥ in and of itself, or it can contain a defect but still be ruled to be ṣaḥīḥ due to supporting evidences.

SALAF: predecessors. Technically used to refer to the best generations of Muslims, the first three generation: the *Ṣaḥābah*, the *Tābiʿūn* and the *Tabʿ Tābiʿūn* due to the ḥadīth, 'The best of people are my generation, then the one that follows, then the one that follows.'

ṢIDQ: truthfulness, the conformity of the inner to the outer such that the deeds and statements of the person do not belie his beliefs and vice-versa. *Ṣidq* is the foundation of faith and results in peace of mind, lying is the foundation of hypocrisy and results in doubt and suspicion, and this is why the two can never co-exist without being at odds with each other. al-Junayd was asked as to whether *ṣidq* and *ikhlāṣ* were the same or different and he replied, 'They are different, *ṣidq* is the root and *ikhlāṣ* is the branch. *Ṣidq* is the foundation of everything and *ikhlāṣ* only comes into play once one commences an action. Actions are only acceptable when they combine both.' The one who has true *ṣidq* will be free of self-conceit.

SHĀDH: irregular, odd. A ḥadīth narrated by a trustworthy and precise narrator that contradicts the narrative of other narrators or the narration of one more trustworthy and precise than him, provided that a reconciliation is not possible.

SHIRK: association, technically referring to directing a right that is due to Allāh Alone to another object of creation, either completely or partially. It can be major (removing a person from the fold of Islām) or minor (not removing a person from the fold of Islām).

SUNNAH: way, path. The actions, words, descriptions, commands, prohibitions and tacit approvals of the Prophet (ﷺ).

TĀBIʿŪN: The generation following that of the Companions.

TABʿ TĀBIʿŪN: The generation following that of the *Tābiʿūn*.

TADLĪS: deceit. An action of a narrator whereby he makes out that he heard something from a particular narrator what he did not hear or conceals the identity of the one he is narrating from. In order to do so, he will use terms that are vague such as 'such-and-such said' and 'on the authority of such-and-such.' The first type of *tadlīs* is blameworthy and constitutes a defect in the *isnād*. The second is dependant upon exactly what was done and the motives of the narrator, it can be blameworthy or not.

TAQWĀ: the basic meaning of which is setting a barrier between two things. This is why it is said that one *ittaqā* with his shield, i.e. he set it as a barrier between him and the one who wished him evil. Therefore it is as if the one who has taqwa (*muttaqī*) has used his following the commands of Allāh and avoiding His prohibitions as a barrier between himself and the Punishment. Hence he has preserved and fortified himself against the punishment of Allāh through his obeying Him.

ṬARQ: the practice of divination through drawing lines in the earth or equally the practice of throwing gravel onto the ground and divination by the shapes subsequently formed therein.

TAWḤĪD: unification, monotheism, the belief in the absolute Oneness of Allāh. It is to believe that Allāh Alone is the creator, nourisher, and sustainer of the worlds; it is to believe that Allāh Alone deserves to be worshipped; and it is to believe that He has unique and perfect Names and Attributes that far transcend anything that one can imagine.

ṬIYARAH: seeing bad omens in things.

WAḤDATU-L-WUJŪD: The unity of existence, the heretical belief that Allāh is everywhere and everything.

WAJD: strong emotion, technically referring to spiritual ecstasy. The heart experiencing sudden surges of intense love, desire, awe and glorification of Allāh.

WARA': pious caution, scrupulousness. A mannerism through which the heart is purified of all that would sully it and has been excellently summarised in the saying of the Prophet (ﷺ), "From the excellence of ones Islām is his leaving that which does not concern him." It is to leave all that causes one doubt, all that does not concern him, to continuously bring oneself to account and to devote oneself to Allāh. Some of the Salaf said, 'None attains the reality of *taqwā* until he leaves that which is harmless for fear of falling into that which is harmful.'

YAQĪN: certainty. It is to faith (*Īmān*) what the soul is to the body, it is the soul to the actions of the heart which in turn formulate the souls to the actions of the limbs and through it one attains the rank of Ṣiddīq. From *yaqīn* does *tawakkul* (absolute reliance in Allāh) sprout and through *yaqīn* is all doubt, suspicion and worry dispelled and the heart filled with love, hope and fear of Allāh. *Yaqīn* is of three levels, that which arises from knowledge (*'ilm al-yaqīn*), seeing (*'ain al-yaqīn*) and actual experience (*Ḥaqq al-yaqīn*).